BOLD

BOLD

NISHA KATONA

Big Flavour Twists to Classic Dishes

NOURISH
EAT WELL   LIVE WELL

FOR MY BOLD PRIDE OF LIONS:
Mini, Beany, The Quen, The Babe,
& The Boy that Climbed with Pine.

ABOUT THE AUTHOR

Nisha Katona gave up a 20-year career as a barrister in 2014 and used all her savings to found and run the Mowgli Street Food restaurants and the Mowgli Trust charity. The Trust raises over £500k each year for charities and sponsors a child in need for every full-time employee. She received an MBE in the 2019 New Year Honours List for services in the food industry. She is the author of five cookbooks including the bestselling *Mowgli Street Food, 30 Minute Mowgli* and *Meat Free Mowgli*. She has been featured extensively as a business and food expert on the BBC, ITV and Channel 4 and Radio 4, and is a regular chef on ITV's *This Morning* and a judge on the BBC's *Great British Menu* and *MasterChef*.

CONTENTS

FORTUNE FAVOURS THE BOLD

INTRODUCTION

'Fortune favours the bold.' I think of this ancient adage as a call to arms. It has been used throughout Western civilisation to emphasise concepts of courage and bravery. Significantly, it is also the motto of Liverpool John Moore's University, of which I am Chancellor. It means those who take risks often reap great rewards – or, to put it another way, be brave when making decisions; push the limits of what you can do. It's a great maxim for life in general, but it's also one that you can – and should – take into the kitchen.

There may be some recipes in this book that will sound wild. There may be some ingredients you've never used before, or flavours that you would never have thought went together. But, trust me on this, that is the whole idea.

Bold is about being brave with your cooking. This book is filled with an eclectic selection of delicious dishes (some familiar, some not; some classics, some new inventions), all made that little bit more exciting by adding new and surprising elements. I want to show you that a little thinking outside the box in the way ingredients are combined can change the way you cook forever.

The way I cook has always been haphazard. I'm a culinary nomad, but I've always been inspired by BIG flavours. Born into an Indian family in the north of England, I learnt to cook our traditional dishes at a young age; I married a Hungarian and discovered the delights of Eastern European cooking; I've travelled the world and expanded my flavour horizons. When I opened my first Mowgli restaurant, I went from the already busy life of a barrister to juggling the even more hectic schedule of a restaurateur; throw in a media career on the side and you find a woman with very little time on her hands for shopping or planning. I have learnt that the contents of a rather empty fridge or barren cupboard coupled with a mad dash to the nearest corner shop can still yield a meal of interest and substance. You just have to think creatively and be a little... bold.

A great example of my approach to cooking is the recipe on page 32 – my Persimmon and Salmon Roe Blinis. These emerged from a real-life scenario of coming home late from filming one day to find no food in the house bar a can of salmon roe in the cupboard and a few persimmons in the fruit bowl, teetering on the edge of freshness. I sliced up the persimmons, opened the can of roe and simply spooned it straight on top of the fruit. The result: a mouthful of heaven. This culinary accident, born out of necessity, is now one of my favourite snacks. And the inspiration for what you are reading now...

It is this spirit of adventure that I want you to embrace. I want you to get adventurous in the kitchen: try new things, new tastes, new techniques, be a little braver. I want you to experience a whole exciting new world of flavour. Leave behind the ordinary – I want you and your friends and family to say 'Wow' next time you sit down to dinner.

—

This collection of recipes all have one thing in common. They all have an element that takes them beyond the usual, the familiar. As well as some exciting, delicious dishes from different world cultures, picked up on my travels and cherished, I have also developed some new versions of old classics, each with a surprising twist to take it out of the ordinary. A chicken burger is given a crunchy-nut makeover and a spicy mayo (page 108); crispy pakoras are filled with haggis (page 28); a mac 'n' cheese has extra oomph from Korean chilli paste and luxurious crab (page 101); oxtail pie is pepped up with coffee (page 124). There are also tantalising sweets and bakes: a fruity malt loaf is spiked with black pepper (see page 135); a sweet fruity pavlova is accompanied by a savoury herbal drizzle that will blow your mind (page 168); a sticky toffee pudding is taken to the next level with a smoky blackstrap molasses sauce (page 174). These are not just twists for the sake of it – they really work and they are all delicious.

There are also some classics from my own heritage that are bold by design. Indians think nothing of adding a touch of chilli to their morning eggs and neither should you (see The Bradford Omelette, page 22). There's a classic Lamb Raan (page 116), whose spiced coating is elevated with a touch of almond-sweet amaretto, that is perfect for entertaining; as is the Kashmiri Crusted Cote de Boeuf (page 130), which is simply to die for. My tasty Chicken and Banana Korma (page 114) is not to be missed at family dinnertime. And the Tomato Ishtew (page 62) is a punchy and nutritious standard from Kerala that will see you right through lunchtime to dinnertime with no mid-afternoon cravings at all. For those who like things on the lighter side, do try the refreshing Watermelon and Alfalfa Chaat (page 52) or the Avo, Basil and Coconut Lassi (page 191) – both are simply mouth-wateringly good.

I'm always instinctive with ingredients. I walk to the market, see what is fresh or cheap that day and take it home confident that I will find a way to make it special. Likewise, store-cupboard staples – cans, packets, jars – are ripe with possibility. I'll often browse the supermarket shelves and just pick up whatever I fancy that looks interesting. Bags of snacking fruit, nuts, a jar of rose harissa..., then I'll get home and wonder what I can do to make them work together. Looking at those larder ingredients got me thinking about how I could use them in different ways – to unlock recipes from around the globe, or to experiment to create something new...

Pick up a bag of dried apricots and you don't just have a cracking treat for snacking on, but also the base for some Middle-Eastern-style Souk Scones (page 152). Dried figs? Into a meatloaf (page 66). That jar of butterscotch sauce you bought for your pancakes – why not try it on your Brussels sprouts (see page 57)? Smoked mackerel for breakfast is lovely, but try it baked into some bread (page 61). Miso paste makes for a delicious soup or stock – but I'll bet you never thought of adding it to a glaze for doughnuts (see page 64).

I have travelled far and wide with these recipes to give you tastes of myriad countries and cultures, dishes that will expand the borders of your flavour comfort zones. With that in mind, there may be ingredients in these pages with which you are unfamiliar – liquorice powder, black salt, dulse, gochujang... and so on. So, in order that the book is truly practical, I have also included a section with some ideas for how you might use these ingredients elsewhere – an ingredient 101 if you will. No one wants to buy an unusual spice or condiment for just one recipe and then never look at it again. I want you to feel empowered to see that jar, can or packet in your cupboard and think: what if I tried it with this... or that? Go to pages 12–19 for the lowdown and get inspired.

—

My first-ever Mowgli restaurant was on Bold Street in Liverpool. We all called it 'Bold' for short. Now, 10 years down the line, we have a growing family of Mowgli restaurants all around the UK, serving the food I love to hungry diners. Back then, people told me I was crazy to risk everything for a restaurant dream, but in my heart it felt that a door in front of me was ajar and I just had to be bold enough to push it open. For me, this was all about faith and the realisation that:

'There is a tide in the affairs of men
Which, taken at the flood, leads on to fortune;
Omitted, all the voyage of their life
Is bound in shallows and in miseries.
On such a full sea are we now afloat;
And we must take the current when it serves,
Or lose our ventures.' *William Shakespeare*

In every way, I wish you fortune – the fortune that favours the bold.

THE WELL-TRAVELLED LARDER

I'm a bit of a shopping nomad. I'm all for shopping the world food aisles in the supermarket and whatever international deli I happen to be passing for cans and jars of weird and wonderful pastes, pickles or preserves; also for packets of dried pasta, beans, fruits. I know they'll keep well and be there for whenever I fancy a bit of kitchen experimentation. But I also know that these things can languish if you don't know what to do with them. In this section you'll find a very brief summary of some of the tasty but maybe more unusual ingredients I've used in this book, and some ideas for where else you might use them.

Here are my top tips for creating a well-travelled larder. Look out for cans or jars of things preserved in oil or in brine – ingredients that will keep well in the cupboard or are inexpensive. Bags of dried snacking fruit are often very economical and can be rehydrated in a little hot water to give you plump fruits to go into stews, or desserts, or even salads. Dried beans, rice and pasta are also on permanent rotation in my kitchen. Cook-from-frozen flatbreads are another great idea – they can be quickly reheated as an accompaniment to so many meals.

Remember you don't have to have a huge range of spices and herbs. Head to pages 18–19 for my essentials for an international spice rack.

Finally, don't forget your fresh ingredients – the jewels that will make the most of these store-cupboard treasures. Shop seasonally. Spend time in the grocers or supermarket working out what's at its peak (or just ask the shopkeeper!). Seasonal shopping means you get fruit and veg when they are at their cheapest. They will also be fresher, having travelled fewer food miles, and therefore will be at their most tasty. Get creative with whatever you find that takes your fancy.

What follows is by no means an exhaustive list, but details just a few of some useful store-cupboard standbys and some lesser-known ingredients that can be helpful to fuel bold culinary adventures.

ANCHOVIES Canned or jarred, these are the ultimate store-cupboard standby for me. There is barely a sauce or dressing that isn't improved by a little added anchovy. Look for ones packed in salt or good olive oil. Use them in a salad Niçoise or Caesar; in tapenade; for a punchy puttanesca sauce (see page 88); draped over pizza; melted over grilled fish or lamb; spread on toast.

CAPERS Having a jar of capers in the cupboard is so useful. Use them to add a tangy, sour and salty flavour to all sorts of Mediterranean-style dishes. These tiny pickled flower buds make a great addition to sauces for fish; they can be sprinkled over pizza; mixed into a remoulade; combined with tuna, lemon juice, olive oil and mayo as a tasty pasta sauce; or popped straight into a tuna salad. Gherkins or even green olives make good substitutes. Rinsing them first will dissipate much of their saltiness.

DULSE (AND OTHER SEAWEEDS) Dulse – sometimes called 'dillisk' – is a red seaweed with a mildly spicy, salted flavour, and is traditionally bought in dried form. It's a well-known snack food in Ireland and can be eaten dried, or soaked in water and added to soups, salads or stir fries. When rehydrated, it is slightly chewy. I've used it to add some seaside flavour to a soda bread on page 61.

FISH SAUCE An essential ingredient in numerous Thai or Vietnamese dishes, fish sauce is also good for making your own dipping sauce for dumplings, fishcakes or fritters. Mix a little into lime juice with a pinch of sugar and some chopped garlic and hot chillies.

GOCHUJANG This savoury, sweet and spicy fermented condiment is popular in Korean cooking. It's basically a chilli paste that can be used (in moderation) as a base for soups, stews, stir frys or marinades, or to pep up burger or taco sauces. You could substitute Sriracha, harissa paste or Thai chilli pastes to similar effect.

KALA NAMAK (BLACK SALT) Also known as Himalayan black salt, this is volcanic rock salt sourced from areas around Asia and the Himalayas and is actually a pinkish colour, not black. It is rather pungently sulfurous in scent and flavour, but is used extensively in India for its medicinal properties, where you will find it added to chutneys, salads, fruit dishes and raitas. Vegans are also known to add a sprinkle to dishes where the flavour of egg is expected or desirable.

KECAP MANIS This is a sweet soy sauce originating in Indonesia. It's thick and syrupy and wonderfully aromatic. I've used it to enrich a flavourful mayo for splurging over a chicken burger (see page 108), but it's also great for balancing the sweetness in Asian dishes when soy sauce would only give you saltiness.

LIQUID SMOKE EXTRACT For that smoky wood-fired flavour without going anywhere near the actual barbecue, liquid smoke can be brushed over burgers, steaks, chicken, vegetables, added to eggs (sparingly) or stirred into baked beans when cooking over a conventional stove. There are various varieties on the market offering you hickory or oak flavours. It can also go into marinades or dips – even into cocktails!

LIQUORICE POWDER Made from ground liquorice root, this is a deliciously different addition to your spice cupboard and it can be used in both sweet and savoury cooking, particularly in baking. It works well in Chinese and Indian savoury dishes (I've used it for a Chinese-style satay on page 40). You could try adding it to a vanilla ice cream base or into the cream for a crème brûlée, or even sprinkling a tiny amount onto other desserts as decoration, where it will add a gentle aniseed flavour. Liquorice also has numerous health benefits and is good for relieving indigestion or soothing a sore throat.

MISO PASTE   For the ultimate in umami, miso paste is your go-to hero. A Japanese fermented soy-bean paste that is increasingly available in mainstream supermarkets these days, miso comes in several styles (red, brown, white, powders and pastes), and all are useful for adding flavour to savoury and sweet dishes. Use it to make a simple, nutritious bowl of miso soup, or work it into marinades for meat or vegetables, gravies or stews, where its yeasty, meaty richness is so comforting and classic. Surprisingly, it also works in sweet contexts, in the way that we now know that adding a little salt to sweet things improves them immeasurably. It goes well with chocolate or caramel, and can even go into ice cream. I've used it in a sweet glaze on savoury doughnuts (page 64) for an intriguing twist on canapés.

'NDUJA   This chilli-hot spreadable sausage paste can be bought in a fresh package in some supermarkets, but also handily comes in a jar, so can be stored in the cupboard and then refrigerated. If you ever see *sobrassada* from Spain or *andouille* from France, they are very similar and can be used in the same ways. Stir it through cooked pasta; add to scrambled or fried eggs, or into an omelette; mix it into bread or scone doughs; stir into soups and stews; spread on toast or crackers. But always remember – it is HOT, so use with caution.

PANDAN (LEAVES/EXTRACT)   Sometimes called screwpine leaves, South-East Asian pandan leaves will add a fragrant sweetness to curries or rice dishes, with hints of vanilla, coconut and rose. Pop a leaf into some steaming rice or wrap meats in leaves before grilling to infuse with flavour. The extract can be combined with coconut milk and used to cook rice too. I've used the extract in a custard (page 160), but it works in baking particularly well, especially added to cake batters, or using it in place of vanilla where you might traditionally use that.

POMEGRANATE MOLASSES   Often called for in Middle-Eastern savoury dishes, particularly lentil stews, a little pomegranate molasses mixed with orange juice and soda water makes a wonderful punch. Or drizzle some over a ham while roasting for a sweetly sour glaze. Add some into dressings or marinades, or drizzle directly over salads or lamb dishes. Brush over halloumi and grill for a quick meze.

PRESERVED LEMONS   These are a super-useful condiment to keep in your larder. Basically a pickle, they will bring salt, acid and umami to the dishes you add it to. It's a classic of North African and Indian cuisines. Use the pulp of preserved lemons, adding it cautiously and tasting as you go as it is very salty, to balance marinades and dressings or even soups and stews. The finely chopped peel can boost a side of green beans or go into a yoghurt for a peppy raita – or cook it low and slow in tagines, stews and bean dishes. You can now also buy jars of preserved lemon paste, which is fab for going straight into salad dressings, sauces and marinades.

SMOKED BUTTER   There are a few varieties of smoked butter available: some in delis (where the butter has a hint of wood-fire smoke); some in the frozen aisle of good supermarkets (where the butter is blended with garlic and smoky paprika). Either way, this rich and decadent ingredient is brilliant for stirring directly through pasta, for topping soup or for melting over roasted or grilled meat or vegetables. Amazing spread on toast, or melted over a baked potato or new potatoes – so many options.

SMOKED SEA SALT   Smoked over a wood fire, this sea salt is a wonderful store-cupboard flavour enhancer for all sorts of dishes – ideal for fooling yourself into believing your food has been cooked over coals. Sprinkle over grilled meats or vegetables before serving to enrich their flavour, or rub into meat or fish before grilling. For just a subtle hint of smokiness, choose a cold-smoked variety; hot-smoked is stronger.

TAHINI   A ground sesame seed paste that is the backbone of numerous Middle-Eastern dishes (think hummus or halva) and works in both savoury and sweet contexts. Add to dips, spreads, sauces, marinades and salad dressings. Asian noodle dishes can also take it as a flavouring. It works well in cookies, cakes and breads, where it combines particularly well with chocolate and honey, or anywhere you might use a nut butter. Store in a cool place or in the refrigerator.

TAMARI   This is a Japanese (and gluten-free) version of soy sauce. Darker, richer and a little less salty than conventional soy sauce, it complements pretty much any savoury dish. Perfect in a salad dressing, or a marinade for chicken, fish or veg.

TAMARIND (FRESH/PASTE)   A common flavouring in South-East Asian and Indian cuisines, sweet and sour tamarind is a fantastic flavouring for curries, chutneys and bean dishes. It comes in several forms: in pods, blocks, slices or concentrates, of which the concentrate is probably the most useful. You can make your own concentrate (there are plenty of tutorials online), but for ease I would always suggest buying the pre-prepared pastes you can now find in supermarkets. Stepping outside of the more conventional curry territory, I've used it to flavour a thirst-quenching cocktail on page 196.

TOASTED SESAME OIL   This intensely nutty-flavoured oil is superb in salad dressings and dipping sauces. It's a very different ingredient to regular sesame oil (which is still a good all-rounder for cooking and for adding a nutty flavour to steamed vegetables, salads or dressings) – its complex, fragrant flavour brings new depth to rice dishes, noodles, stir fries or grilled vegetables, where it should be drizzled over raw just before serving (never cooked, which would make it bitter).

WASABI (POWDER/PASTE)   An essential ingredient for anyone who loves Japanese food, wasabi products are notoriously strongly flavoured, so use in moderation. Use to bring heat to dipping sauces or to season sushi. I've used it to pep up a guacamole on page 46 and to bring some heat to a fish gratin on page 104. Related to horseradish, so naturally it is also wonderful with beef – you can make a quick marinade for steak by mixing a pinch with a little rice vinegar and soy sauce.

CHILLIES 101

The bold ingredient extraordinaire, I've used an exciting, global selection of chillies in this book. Here is a brief lowdown on some of the different types available (just the ones I've chosen to use in this book – there are hundreds of varieties out there...) and what they can bring to your cooking. As well as in delis, you'll often find dried chillies available in packets online. Usually, you'll have some left over. Knowing what else they are great for will hopefully inspire you to experiment with them in other dishes. Once you have found a variety you love, also buy them in the form of dried flakes – adding a pinch wherever you want some heat.

FRESH OR DRIED

ANCHO   The dried version of a poblano green chilli pepper, ancho is a mild, sweet, fruity chilli and one of the most commonly used varieties in Mexican cuisine. It has notes of bitter chocolate and dried fruit and is not too hot. Buy dried and use in salsas, mole stews or chile con carne.

BIRD'S-EYE   These Thai chillies have a pungent heat quite out of proportion to their diminutive size. They bring a fiery, fruity bite to southeast Asian dishes, such as curries or soups. Or try them in Indian pickles. Go easy when adding them and build up gradually to your preferred level of heat. Use gloves when preparing them to protect your eyes from their burning juices.

CHIPOTLE   Another Mexican chilli, the chipotle is smoky and medium–hot. It is a jalapeño chilli that has been dried over wood smoke, which is what gives it such a warm depth of flavour. Use in slow-cooked dishes such as mole. I buy chipotle chilli flakes and use in Mexican-style spice rubs for chicken and other meats.

GREEN (INDIAN VARIETIES)   Indian green finger chillies are the type most commonly used to bring not just heat to dishes, but a zingy, green, vegetal freshness. Pierce them and throw in whole with the dried spices for flavour but not so much heat; chop them up and add for both heat and freshness. To reduce their heat, remove the pith and seeds. As a general rule, the thinner the chilli, the hotter it is. Larger banana chillies are good for mild flavour, but you may need to add more to get the right amount of zing in your dishes.

GUAJILLO   Used in my Mole Meatballs (page 127), dried guajillo chillies are mild–medium hot and have a lovely bright, tangy flavour. Buy them dried and toast in a dry pan to release their flavours before rehydrating to use in dishes. They will work well in any Mexican dish with a spicy sauce.

JALAPEÑOS   A medium–hot Spanish or South American chilli, this is what you might use when a recipe calls for 'chilli' without being more specific. Sold in both green and red forms (the red is riper and slightly sweeter), they are a good workhorse chilli for fruity flavour and subtle heat.

KASHMIRI   These beautiful Indian chillies bring a vibrant red hue to any dish you use them in as well as delicious flavour. They are very mild, so are perfect if you are looking for a gentler heat. Soak in hot water and purée or simply chop and add to curry pastes. As well as dried, I use them in powdered form – a pinch of Kashmiri chilli powder will bring intense colour, but mild heat to dishes. As well as in curries, or mixed into yoghurt for a colourful marinade, try sprinkling over your eggs in the morning or stirring into a tomatoey pasta sauce.

RED (INDIAN VARIETIES)   There are so many varieties of red Indian chilli that it is impossible to give a full picture here, but in short we use small dried red chillies to bring a gentle heat to dishes.

Longer dried red chillies bring more smoky flavour than heat. Both are fried in hot oil at the start of preparing dishes for subtle fire. Fresh red chillies come in many forms and heat levels; the smaller and thinner the chilli, the hotter it may be. Add wherever you want fresh fruity flavour and a little fire. Fabulous in pickles and salsas.

SCOTCH BONNET   Fruity and fiery, the Scotch bonnet is an essential part of West Africa and Caribbean cuisines. It's not for the faint of heart – it will bring some serious heat to whatever you add it to, but it also brings a tropical fruitiness with it that I love. Add to jerk-style dishes, tomato stews, salsas and marinades. It also makes a good substitute for habanero peppers if you have a recipe that requires them. Take care when preparing them as their chilli fire can burn if it gets into your eyes – wear gloves and googles if you plan to chop them up.

SAUCES & PASTES

SRIRACHA SAUCE   This bright-red hot chilli sauce hails from Thailand, but you can now find good imitations made all over the world. Made from chillies, vinegar, garlic, salt and sugar, it will add a pungent kick to any meal. It is not quite as hot as Tabasco sauce, but is stronger than many hot sauces. Add as a spicy condiment to tacos, wraps, burgers, to mayonnaise or salad dressings, drizzle on fried eggs or avocado on toast, or add to a batch of popcorn for a moreish and exciting snack.

AJÍ AMARILLO PASTE   A bright orange-yellow chilli paste from Peru that is aromatic and slightly fruity. Medium spicy, it makes a great base for Latin American stews, marinades and dressings, or for ceviche. I use it in Halloumi Saltado (page 92).

ANCHO CHILLI PASTE   Tangy, smoky chilli paste that is a good time saver in recipes that call for ancho chillies (see opposite). Use in Mexican-style sauces, stews and marinades, or as a hot drizzle for tacos. See also my Mole Meatballs (page 127).

GOCHUJANG   A Korean paste that is spicy, savoury, sweet and slightly funky. It gets its unique flavour from the slow, years-long fermentation process of gochugaru (chilli powder), glutinous rice, fermented soybean powder and salt. The result is a thick, sticky, deep-red paste that can be used in marinades, dipping sauces, soups and stews for a sweet and hot tang. A little goes a long way and it will need to be thinned out in some liquid so that it doesn't burn during cooking.

HARISSA PASTE   This North African roasted red pepper paste is aromatic and herbal as well as spicy. It is widely used in Moroccan and Middle Eastern cuisines for mild heat and rich flavour. Add to stews and tagines, rub onto meat or fish before grilling or roasting, mix into meatballs or burger patties, add to soup, run through hummus, add to mayo or serve as a condiment. It's super versatile. Also available is rose harissa, made with rose petals, that brings a delicate floral fragrance to dishes and balances out the heat of the chillies a little.

THE INTERNATIONAL SPICE RACK

More than the classic Indian collection, these spices will take your culinary adventures global. This is not an exhaustive list – by all means expand your horizons further. Just remember, don't buy large amounts of spices that you are not going to use up. It can be more economical to buy in bulk, but if you don't use them frequently and within a year, they will just go off. With these in your cupboard you can cook any dish in this book... and more.

ALLSPICE   Ground allspice is slightly bitter, earthy and fruity – it tastes like a combination of cloves, cinnamon and nutmeg all rolled into one. A wintery spice that you might find in gingerbread, it's also a key component of jerk marinades.

AMCHOOR   Also known as amchur, this is dried green mango powder. It brings a citrussy, sweet-and-sour hit to dishes and is commonly used in Indian cuisine as a sharpening tangy flavour, much as we might use lemon or lime to finish a dish.

BLACK MUSTARD SEEDS   Pungent and distinctive, the spicy nuttiness of black mustard seeds will bring a bold note to any curry dish when fried in hot oil.

CAJUN SPICE BLEND   This blend of spices from Louisiana combines paprika, chilli and garlic powder amongst other things to produce a smoky, spicy seasoning ideal for rice dishes, soups, marinades and as a rub for meat or fish.

CARDAMOM PODS   I like to use both the green pods and the smoky black ones. A few black cardamom pods added to the pot when cooking basmati will produce a wonderfully aromatic rice.

The ground seeds of green pods bring a sweet aromatic pungency to desserts and drinks too.

CAYENNE PEPPER   A moderately hot chilli powder that is lightly sweet with a subtle smokiness and fresh red pepper flavour.

CHAAT MASALA   A funky mix of amchoor, cumin, coriander/cilantro, ginger, salt, pepper and chilli powder, this is a moreish zingy spice blend that perks up many Indian snack dishes. Add a pinch or two to sliced fruits to liven them up.

CHILLI POWDERS (MILD AND HOT)   Chilli powder brings a smoky heat and should be used in moderation – build it up gradually to get the level of heat you want. I love using Kashmiri chilli powder for its intense red colour.

CHINESE FIVE SPICE   This Asian seasoning is a mix of star anise, cloves, cinnamon, Sichuan peppercorns and fennel seeds. It is a combination of all five tastes – sweet, sour, bitter, salty and umami. Useful in all kinds of Chinese or Taiwanese cooking, in stews or for meat marinades.

CLOVES   Used whole or ground, this pungent

spice is sweet and spicy and should be used sparingly. Use to flavour curries, baked hams, drinks and syrups.

CORIANDER/CILANTRO (SEEDS/GROUND)
I find this spice subtle but essential, bringing a delicate, herbal note to curries. I particularly use it as a finishing note for vegetable dishes.

CUMIN (SEEDS/GROUND)   This punchy spice will always bring added oomph to any curry. Fry the deeply flavourful seeds at the beginning of cooking a dish to transform them from bitter to citrussy and almost woody in flavour.

DRIED CHILLI (HOT PEPPER) FLAKES   Discover your favourite chilli (pages 16–17) and buy it in dried flaked form to add whenever and wherever you want a hit of heat in your cooking.

DRIED CURRY LEAVES   Citrussy, with hints of lemongrass and nuttiness, dried curry leaves can be added to dals, curries, fried vegetable dishes, soups, stir fries and more. Fry in hot oil first to release their aromas.

FENNEL (SEEDS/GROUND)   Delivering a sweet, powerful hit of liquorice to dishes, this is a beautiful spice to have in your cupboard. Dry fry to enhance their flavour before using.

GARAM MASALA   The ultimate spice for meat dishes, this blend of up to 20 different spices is worth buying in bulk and using frequently. Add it at the end of cooking a curry as a finishing flavour.

NIGELLA SEEDS   Wonderful when combined with fresh green chillies, these little black seeds should be fried in hot oil at the start of making a dish and bring an earthy hit of flavour.

NUTMEG (FRESH/GROUND)   Woody, nutty and slightly sweet, this wintery spice works in both sweet and savoury dishes for comforting warmth and aroma. Use sparingly as a little goes a long way.

PANCH PHORON   Known as Bengali 'five spice', this is an enigmatic combination of cumin, fenugreek, nigella and mustard seeds, and often fennel seeds. Typically, Indians will fry this off at the start of making a curry and it brings a nuanced, heady flavour that I adore.

PINK PEPPERCORNS   With a much brighter, fruitier and milder flavour than black peppercorns, you are sure to find many uses for this spice. Use in buttery sauces, salads and dressings, and with seafood or poultry.

SAFFRON   The vivid crimson threads of saffron are sweet, floral and earthy. Expensive and delicate, use sparingly in paella, bouillabaisse, risotto, mild curries or even in baking.

STAR ANISE   This spice has a distinct liquorice-like flavour. Use it in Asian dishes, particularly those of Chinese or Vietnamese origin for a hit of fresh pungency.

SUMAC   Tart and sharp, this deep red spice is citrussy and reminiscent of fresh lemon juice. A pinch will liven up most dishes, particularly those of Middle Eastern origin.

PAPRIKA (SWEET/ SMOKED/HOT)   Another ground red pepper spice, its heat is generally mild and it can be used to complement many dishes, especially Spanish (think paella), Hungarian (think goulash) or other Eastern European dishes. Sweet paprika is more fruity in tone, and smoked paprika obviously brings a hit of woodiness. Hot paprika is made with extra-spicy red peppers, so use a bit more sparingly.

TURMERIC (GROUND)   This deep golden-orange spice is one of the major building blocks of any curry, providing an earthy, peppery base flavour. It is also anti-inflammatory and a mood enhancer – I use it a lot. Add it with softer/wetter ingredients to avoid burning it.

SMALL PLATES

THE BRADFORD OMELETTE

Take the humble omelette and give it some oomph with cumin seeds, verdant coriander and the fresh clean heat of green chilli to wake you up of a morning. The city of Bradford in the north of England has a huge Asian population. I spent a lot of time there with friends as a child and this is what we would often have for breakfast. Indians think nothing of adding a bit of bold heat to their morning eggs. For a more substantial meal, you could add some cooked potatoes inside the omelette (together with the onion and spices, they would taste similar to Bombay potatoes). With some hot buttered toast on the side and a cup of chai, this makes a great start to the day. The real heat fiends among you can take things up another level with a few drops of your favourite chilli oil to serve.

1 tbsp vegetable oil

½ tsp cumin seeds

1 small onion, finely sliced

1 green chilli, finely chopped

4 eggs

½ tsp ground coriander

½ tsp ground turmeric

a large pinch of sea salt

60g/2oz Cheddar cheese, finely grated

To serve:

fresh coriander/cilantro leaves

sliced green chilli

chilli oil

Heat the oil in a non-stick frying pan over a medium heat and add the cumin seeds. Cook them until fragrant and deep brown in colour, then add the onion and green chilli, and cook for 10 minutes until the onion is beginning to caramelise. Tip onto a plate and set aside.

In a bowl, beat the eggs together with the ground coriander, turmeric and a large pinch of salt.

Pour the eggs into the hot pan and give it all a quick mix. Cook until the eggs are half set, then sprinkle the onion mixture over the top of the omelette along with the grated cheese. Leave to cook until the eggs are almost set, then flip in half and cook until the cheese is bubbling at the edges.

Transfer to a plate, sprinkle with chopped coriander and green chilli, and serve with your favourite chilli oil.

SPECKLED SPICED SCOTCH EGGS

These Scotch eggs have a secret warming garam masala spicing in the pork coating as well as an attractive speckled appearance from the nigella seeds. Don't just save them for picnics, they make a beautiful starter course served with some fresh herbs or salad, perhaps with a tomato salsa or chutney on the side.

2 tbsp olive oil

1 large onion, finely diced

2 tbsp store-bought ginger paste

2 tbsp store-bought garlic paste

1 tbsp paprika

3 tsp nigella seeds

2 tbsp garam masala

9 eggs (the nice golden-yolked ones are best for this)

500g/1lb 2oz minced/ground pork

2 tsp fine salt

150g/5oz/1½ cups breadcrumbs

3 tbsp plain/all-purpose flour

sunflower or vegetable oil, for frying

freshly ground black pepper

Heat the olive oil in a frying pan and add the onion. Cook over a low–medium heat for 8–10 minutes, stirring occasionally, until the onions are cooked and beginning to colour. Add the ginger and garlic pastes, the paprika, 1 teaspoon of the nigella seeds and the garam masala and cook for a few more minutes, then set aside to cool.

Bring a large pan of water to the boil and add six of the eggs. Boil for 6 minutes (longer if you don't want the yolks runny) then remove them with a slotted spoon and put them straight into a bowl of cold water to cool completely. Once cool, peel them very carefully as they will still be a bit soft and wobbly.

Put the pork in a large bowl and add the cooked spiced onions and salt. Beat one of the remaining eggs and add it to the pork, then mix well until everything is completely combined. Divide the mixture into six equal balls.

In a shallow dish, mix the breadcrumbs with the remaining 2 teaspoons of nigella seeds. Beat the remaining two eggs and put them in another shallow dish, then put the flour in a third dish, seasoning it with black pepper. Take a ball of the pork mixture and press it out over the palm of your hand to form a thin patty in your palm – make it as big as you can, as it needs to be large enough to surround the entire egg. With your other hand, take an egg and coat it in flour, then place it onto the pork and pull the pork around it. Use both hands to even out the layer of meat, smoothing it over and making sure the egg is totally enclosed. Set aside while you cover the other eggs in the same way.

Heat enough sunflower or vegetable oil for deep frying in a deep, heavy pan to 160°C/325°F.

One by one, dip the eggs first in the flour, then in the egg and finally in the breadcrumbs. Roll them around in each coating so that they are evenly covered before you move on to the next. Lower the eggs into the hot oil with a slotted spoon and fry them for about 7 minutes until crisp and golden on the outside. You may have to do this in batches as they are quite big once coated and you don't want to overcrowd the pan or they won't brown evenly. Once golden, remove the eggs from the oil with a slotted spoon and transfer to a plate lined with paper towels to drain.

Eat warm or leave to cool completely.

WILD WELSH RAREBIT

Even old stalwarts can benefit from the bold treatment. A hit of chilli, the subtle fragrance of ground coriander and the green grassiness of fresh coriander livens up the classic Welsh rarebit. Cheese on toast never tasted so good.

40g/1½oz butter
1 small red onion, finely diced
2 tsp ground coriander
1 green chilli and 1 red chilli, deseeded and finely diced
  (leave the seeds in if you'd like it hotter)
200ml/7fl oz/scant 1 cup semi-skimmed milk
40g/1½oz/⅓ cup plain/all-purpose flour
250g/9oz mature Cheddar cheese, grated
1 tsp English mustard
a large handful of fresh coriander/cilantro,
  roughly chopped
4 large, thick slices (or 8 smaller ones) of crusty bread
salt and freshly ground black pepper

Melt 1 tablespoon of the butter in a small frying pan over a low–medium heat and add the onion and ground coriander. Cook for at least 8 minutes until the onion has caramelised, then add the green and red chillies and cook for another couple of minutes. Remove from the heat and set aside.

Warm the milk slightly in the microwave.

Melt the remaining butter in a saucepan over a low heat. Add the flour and cook for a few minutes, stirring regularly, to cook out the flavour of the flour. A little at a time, add the warm milk to the pan, whisking well between each addition, until you have a smooth roux with no lumps. Continue cooking the sauce for a few minutes over a medium heat until it begins to thicken, then add the cheese and stir in until melted. Add the mustard along with the onion and chilli mixture and stir. Taste and season with salt and pepper, then stir in most of the fresh coriander, reserving a little for garnish.

Preheat the grill/broiler to medium and toast the bread slices on both sides until lightly golden. Remove from the grill and spread the sauce generously over the slices. Return them to the grill for a few minutes until golden and bubbling on top, then serve sprinkled with the remaining coriander.

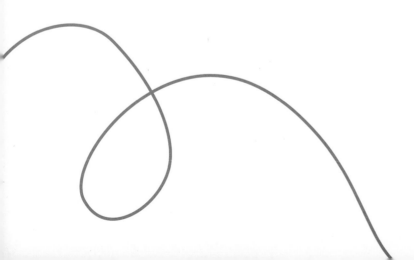

HAGGIS PAKORAS

Anyone who has visited an Indian or Pakistani restaurant in Scotland recently might have seen this specialty on the menu: haggis pakoras. A truly Scottish twist on classic Indian fare, it really works, as haggis (both the meat and veggie versions) makes a brilliant candidate for deep frying. I thought I'd put a Glaswegian spin on things by enfolding the haggis in a batter imbued with every Scotsman's favourite soft drink: Irn Bru. These punchy bites are delicious served with a tomato chutney on the side and guaranteed to put hairs on your chest, or at least create a talking point to kick off dinner. And if you don't fancy the Irn Bru, try replacing it with the same quantity of beer or lager, which will work just as well.

450g/1lb haggis
190g/6½oz/1¾ cups gram flour/besan
½ tsp bicarbonate of soda/baking soda
½ tsp chilli powder
1 tsp ground turmeric
1½ tsp garam masala
½ tsp salt
about 300ml/10fl oz/1¼ cups Irn Bru (or beer or lager)
   (you may not need it all)
vegetable oil, for deep frying

Remove the casing from the haggis and crumble it up into largish chunks in a small bowl. Set aside.

In another bowl, mix together the gram flour, bicarbonate of soda, spices and salt. Slowly pour in the Iru Bru, stirring as you go. You need it to form a smooth, thick paste, so add the liquid slowly and stop adding if the batter's getting too loose. Once you have a thick batter that pours at a slow ooze, stir in the haggis chunks.

Pour the oil into a saucepan to a depth of about 5cm/2in and heat to 180°C/350°F (or heat a deep-fat fryer to the same temperature). If you don't have a kitchen thermometer, the oil is hot enough when a small amount of batter sizzles and floats to the surface when dropped in.

Scoop tablespoons of the batter and carefully dollop them straight into the hot oil. Cook just a few at a time so you don't overcrowd the pan and they can crisp up nicely. Cook for 3–5 minutes until golden and crisp. Remove from the oil with a slotted spoon and leave to drain on a plate lined with paper towels while you cook the remaining batches. Serve hot.

DEMONS ON HORSEBACK

The original 'devils on horseback' are dates, stuffed with cheese or nuts and wrapped in bacon. I've altered the recipe slightly to make them truly demonic – with Sriracha sauce for some explosive heat and a cute sweety drop pepper in place of the cheese or nuts. The ideal canapé for a pepper-loving fiend.

24 large pitted prunes
4 tbsp Sriracha sauce
24 jarred sweety drop peppers, drained
12 rashers streaky bacon, sliced in half lengthways

Soak some wooden cocktail sticks/toothpicks in water for about 30 minutes (so they don't burn under the grill).

Cut a small slit in the side of each prune (if there's not an obvious hole where the stone was removed). Spoon ½ teaspoon of the Sriracha sauce into each prune, then pop a whole tiny pepper into the hole. Take a length of bacon and wrap it around the prune, then secure it in place with one of the soaked cocktail sticks. Repeat to fill and wrap all the prunes.

Preheat the grill/broiler to medium–high. Pop the demons on a baking sheet and place under the grill. Cook for about 8–9 minutes, turning during cooking, or until the bacon is golden and crispy on all sides.

Arrange your demons on a serving platter and serve warm.

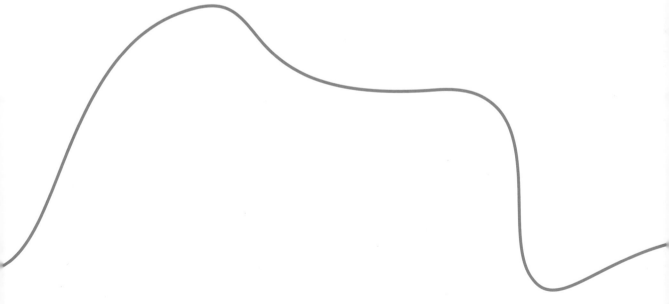

PERSIMMON AND SALMON ROE BLINIS

I invented this combination entirely by accident when, coming home late one evening to a refrigerator bare save a can of salmon roe and some persimmons in the fruit bowl, I decided to slice up the persimmon and eat with a spoonful of roe on top. I loved it so much it has since become a favourite snack. It makes a brilliant canapé to serve with drinks, that zing of orange colour making them an irresistible beacon to which all are drawn like moths to a flame.

1 large persimmon
1 pack of 24 canapé blinis
100g/3½oz crème fraîche
a bag of watercress
40g/1½oz salmon roe
freshly ground black pepper

Slice the persimmon into 5mm/¼in thick slices – you should make six slices, excluding the ends – then quarter each one so you have 24 little wedges.

Warm the blinis according to the packet instructions, then top each one with a wedge of persimmon.

Spoon 1 teaspoon of crème fraîche on top of the persimmon and grind over a little black pepper, then top that with a dainty sprig of watercress.

Finally, spoon a teaspoon of the salmon roe over the top of each blini.

Arrange them on a platter and serve immediately.

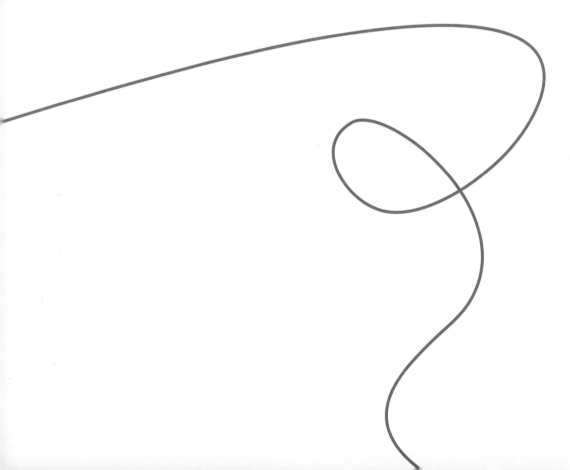

POPPING SPICE MONKFISH SCAMPI
WITH COCONUT AND CHILLI RAITA

Scampi with a difference. I love the combination of spices in the batter of these little morsels. There was a time when monkfish was seen as a cheaper substitute for real scampi, but now the meaty texture of monkfish is prized and it's definitely a more luxurious treat. Tasty, tender and moreish, and with a flavoursome creamy yet zingy coconut raita on the side, these really do pop.

2 tsp coriander seeds

1 tsp cumin seeds

1 tsp fennel seeds

1 tsp nigella seeds

½ tsp black mustard seeds

about 600ml/20fl oz/2½ cups light-flavoured oil (such as vegetable or sunflower), for deep frying

150g/5oz/1¼ cups plain/all-purpose flour, plus extra for dusting

200g/7oz/generous 1¾ cups gram flour/besan

¾ tsp bicarbonate of soda/baking soda

½ tsp salt

350ml/12fl oz/scant 1½ cups sparkling water

500g/1lb 2oz monkfish, diced into large cubes

lemon wedges, to serve

For the coconut, chilli and coriander dip:

70g/2½oz fresh coconut

5cm/2in chunk of cucumber, roughly chopped

2 tbsp fresh lime juice (about 1 lime)

a small bunch of fresh coriander/cilantro

a small handful of fresh mint

2 tsp caster/superfine sugar

4 tbsp thick Greek yogurt

1 green chilli, deseeded and diced

1 tsp sea salt

First make the dip. Remove any tough brown skin from the coconut, then roughly chop it and place in a mini chopper or the small bowl of a food processor along with the cucumber. Add the lime juice and blitz until the coconut is a rough crumb. Add the herbs and sugar, and blitz again until you have a paste. Stir the paste into the yogurt along with the diced green chilli, taste and season with the salt. Put in the refrigerator until ready to serve.

Put the spice seeds into a dry frying pan and toast over a medium heat until they smell aromatic and the cumin seeds have turned a deep brown colour. Tip them onto a plate and leave to cool. Once cool, crack the spices in a pestle and mortar, or with a rolling pin, leaving them reasonably coarse.

Before mixing the batter (as you will need to use it quite fast), get the oil heating to 180°C/350°F in a deep-fat fryer or large saucepan.

Meanwhile, sift the flours and bicarbonate of soda into a bowl. Add the toasted spices and season well with salt, then pour in the sparkling water and whisk until there are no lumps and the batter is smooth.

Tip a little flour onto a plate and add a few of the monkfish pieces, rolling them around to coat. Once floured, dip them into the batter to fully coat and then carefully drop them into the hot oil. Cook them a few at a time (if you overcrowd the pan, they will go soggy) for about 3 minutes, or until the monkfish is cooked and the batter is crisp and golden. Fish them out with a slotted spoon and drain on paper towels while you cook the rest in batches.

Serve the bites hot with the coconut dip and lemon wedges for squeezing.

BENGALI HASH BROWNS

A combination of classic American hash browns with the spiced *aloo chop* cutlets of Bengal, I like to serve these potato cakes as a snack with a refreshing yoghurty raita, and a nice chutney works well too.

vegetable oil, for frying
1½ tsp panch phoron/Bengali 'five spice'
2 small onions, finely sliced
650g/1lb 7oz potatoes (a floury sort will work well for extra crispiness)
2 green chillies, finely sliced (leave the seeds in)
1 small egg, beaten
salt and black pepper
raita and/or chutney, to serve

Heat a sauté pan (or a deep frying pan) over a low–medium heat and add 2 tablespoons of oil. Fry the panch phoron and onions for 10 minutes until the onions are soft and beginning to caramelise. Leave to cool.

While the onion is cooling, peel and grate your potatoes and tip them onto a clean dish towel. Gather up the edges of the towel and squeeze over the sink to remove any excess moisture from the potatoes, then add them to a large bowl. Tip the cooked onion into the bowl, followed by the chillies and beaten egg. Season generously and mix everything together.

Wipe out the frying pan with a bit of paper towel. Add more oil to the pan to a depth of about 1cm/½in and heat over a medium–high heat. Scoop amounts of the potato mixture (each about the size of a golf ball) and roll into balls, then flatten them a little to form patties of an even thickness. Once the oil is hot and shimmering, and working in batches, cook several of the patties in the hot oil for a few minutes until browning well underneath. Once cooked on the bottom, flip them over with a spatula and cook until the other side is well browned. Remove them from the hot oil and leave to drain on paper towels while you fry the rest.

Serve hot with raita or chutney for dipping.

CHERMOULA POTTED SHRIMP

WITH CARROT AND PRESERVED LEMON PICKLE

As an occasional treat, I love a pot of the famous delicately spiced Morecambe Bay potted shrimps, and they are very easy to make yourself at home too. For my own bolder recipe, I add a touch of Moroccan chermoula spices to the shrimp, then serve with plenty of crusty sourdough with a punchy pickle on the side. Serve as an elegant starter when entertaining friends and family, then close your eyes and feel transported from the chilly bays of Lancashire to the more glamorous climes of Casablanca.

120g/4oz good salted butter
200g/7oz brown shrimp
8 slices of sourdough bread

For the chermoula paste:
½ garlic clove, finely chopped
a good pinch of flaky sea salt
a large handful each of fresh coriander/cilantro and
  parsley, chopped, plus extra to serve
½ tsp ground cumin
½ tsp sweet paprika
¼ tsp ground turmeric
grated zest and juice of ½ lemon
1 tsp olive oil

For the carrot and preserved lemon pickle:
½ tsp cumin seeds
75ml/2½fl oz/5 tbsp cider vinegar
80g/3oz/⅓ cup caster/superfine sugar
2 large carrots (about 250g/9oz in total),
  peeled and grated
1 preserved lemon, pips removed, finely diced
2cm/¾in piece of fresh ginger, peeled and grated
½ red chilli, finely diced
1 garlic clove, grated
salt, to taste

To make the chermoula paste, put the garlic and a good pinch of salt in a pestle and mortar and pound to a paste. Add the coriander and parsley and pound again until it is broken down into a paste, then stir in the dried spices, lemon zest and juice, and oil.

Melt the butter for the potted shrimp gently in a saucepan, then turn off the heat. Stir in the chermoula paste, then, once incorporated, stir in the shrimp. Scoop the shrimp out of the pan using a slotted spoon, to leave most of the butter in the pan, and divide the shrimp evenly among four ramekin dishes, pressing them down gently to level the tops. Pour over the remaining butter and place them in the refrigerator to set completely.

Meanwhile, make the pickle. Put the cumin seeds in a dry saucepan and toast over a low heat until fragrant and deep brown in colour. Add the vinegar and sugar, and stir until the sugar has dissolved. Add the remaining ingredients and stir everything together well. Simmer over a medium heat for 10 minutes, stirring occasionally. Taste and season with salt, then leave to cool completely. This will keep in a jar in the refrigerator for a week.

When you are ready to serve, toast the bread slices and serve them with the little pots of shrimps and carrot pickle, for spreading onto the toasts. Scatter over some extra parsley for a bit of colour if you like.

LIQUORICE AND ALMOND CHICKEN SATAY

Switching out the curry in traditional satay for the anise flavours of liquorice takes this dish a little more north of its Indonesian home to China, for a deeper, richer flavour, so I have swapped the traditional peanuts and coconut in the sauce for almond butter. Delicious. Note that you will need eight wooden skewers.

3 large chicken breasts
olive oil, for cooking

For the marinade:
2 large garlic cloves, crushed
2.5cm/1in piece of fresh root ginger, peeled and grated
1 tbsp liquorice powder
4 tbsp dark soy sauce
2 tbsp rice wine
½ tsp ground cinnamon
a large pinch of sea salt

For the satay dipping sauce:
60g/2oz almond butter
1 tbsp dark soy sauce
2½ tsp liquorice powder
½ red chilli, finely diced
1 tbsp honey
3 tbsp lemon juice
sea salt, to taste

To serve:
little gem lettuce
sliced red chilli
30g/1oz flaked almonds, toasted
sea salt flakes

Put eight wooden skewers to soak in some water.

Cut the chicken into long strips, each a few millimetres thick, down the length of each breast. Combine all the ingredients for the marinade in a large bowl and add the chicken strips. Stir so that all the chicken is well coated, then cover and leave to marinate in the refrigerator for a few hours.

Meanwhile, make the dipping sauce by combining all the ingredients in a bowl. Season to taste with salt.

Once the chicken has marinated, thread the strips of chicken onto the soaked skewers, looping the strips back and forth over the point of the skewers to weave the strips on. Don't push the chicken together too tightly or it won't cook properly.

Preheat a ridged stovetop griddle/grill pan over a medium–high heat and grease it with a little oil. Place the skewers on the griddle (you may have to cook them in batches, depending on the size of your griddle) and cook for about 6 minutes in total, turning regularly, until they are golden brown on all sides, have charred lines from the griddle and the chicken is cooked through.

Arrange the skewers on a bed of lettuce and drizzle with a little of the satay sauce. Sprinkle with the chilli, toasted almonds and sea salt flakes and serve with the remaining sauce on the side for dipping.

ANCHOVY AND CHEESY PINEAPPLE CROQUETAS

Trust me, this is such a great recipe. One of my most controversial recipe hits has always been my anchovy and pineapple arancini, fusing sweet-and-sour Vietnamese flavours with Italian rice balls, so I've taken that basic idea and ran with it a little further. Zinging up the blandness of plain croquetas and playing on a seventies cheese and pineapple theme, these little cocktail bites have that secret hit of anchovy and chilli pepping them up and plenty of ooze.

For the filling:
2 canned pineapple rings
75g/2½oz butter
100g/3½oz/generous ¾ cup plain/all-purpose flour
450ml/15fl oz/1¾ cups whole milk
100g/3½oz Cheddar cheese, grated
1 x 50g/2oz can anchovies, fillets drained
   and chopped
1 red chilli, finely diced (leave the seeds in)
½ tsp salt (or to taste)

For coating and cooking:
80g/3oz/⅔ cup plain/all-purpose flour
2 eggs, beaten
150g/5oz/2 cups fresh breadcrumbs (made from
   stale white crumbs)
vegetable or sunflower oil, for deep frying

Drain the pineapple rings and finely dice them. Set them aside on paper towels to drain a little more.

Meanwhile, melt the butter in a saucepan over a low–medium heat, then add the flour. Cook for a couple of minutes, then begin adding the milk a little at a time, whisking well between each addition to get rid of any lumps. Once all the milk is added, add the cheese and increase the heat to medium.

Cook for about 5 minutes, stirring constantly, until the flour flavour has gone and the mixture is very thick and coming away from the pan, like choux pastry. Stir in the anchovies, diced pineapple, chilli and salt, then pour the mixture into a bowl or ceramic baking dish and cover the surface of the bechamel with a piece of cling film/plastic wrap. Leave to cool, then place in the refrigerator overnight to set firmly.

The next day, shape your croquetas. Liberally dust a baking sheet with some of the flour, then take 2 dessertspoons and use them to scoop and shape your croquetas, dropping the shaped ones onto the baking sheet and shaking gently to cover in flour. Repeat until all the mixture is used up – you should have around 20. Pop them back in the refrigerator while you set up a production line.

Put the remaining flour on a plate, the beaten eggs into a shallow bowl and the breadcrumbs onto another plate. Fill a deep saucepan or deep-fat fryer half full with oil and pop it on the hob/stovetop to heat up to 180°C/350°F.

Working with about four or five croquetas at a time so that you don't overcrowd your pan, dunk them first in the flour, then in the egg and finally in the breadcrumbs, making sure they are fully covered at each stage. Lower them into the hot oil with a slotted spoon and cook for 2–3 minutes until lightly golden and their bechamel centres are molten. While one batch is cooking, start coating the next batch.

Once cooked, fish the croquetas out of the oil and leave to drain on paper towels for a couple of minutes before serving. Repeat to cook the whole batch and enjoy while still warm.

LANDED GENTRY POTSTICKERS

The very British ingredients that are parsnip and venison pair beautifully with Asian flavours for these dumplings with a twist. I can imagine these being made for a weekend party at a country house – the Nepalese chef in the kitchen whipping up some magic with aristocratic ingredients to impress those in the dining room. These are seriously moreish and make a great lunch dish on their own or a perfect prelude to an Asian fusion feast.

150g/5oz minced/ground venison

sunflower or vegetable oil, for frying

100g/3½oz chestnut/cremini mushrooms, finely chopped (or use shiitake if you're feeling fancy)

75g/2½oz parsnip, peeled and grated

3 spring onions/scallions, finely sliced, plus extra to serve

about 24 round gyoza wrappers

For the marinade:

1½ tbsp kecap manis

2 tsp panch phoron/Bengali 'five spice'

1 garlic clove, finely chopped

2cm/¾in piece of fresh root ginger, grated

1 tsp fish sauce

1 tsp rice vinegar

1 tsp sesame oil

½–1 red chilli, finely diced (depending on how much of a tingle you want)

a pinch of salt

For the dipping sauce:

2 tbsp soy sauce

2 tsp toasted sesame oil

2 tsp rice vinegar

1 tsp sesame seeds

Mix together all the ingredients for the marinade, add the venison and set aside.

Heat about 1 tablespoon of oil in a large frying pan over a medium–high heat. Fry the mushrooms for 4 minutes or so until starting to brown and reduce down, then add the parsnip and cook for a couple of minutes. Add the spring onions and give the mixture a final minute. Leave to cool a little, then tip into the bowl with the venison mixture and stir together well.

To assemble, place a dumpling wrapper in the palm of your hand and use your finger dipped in water to dampen the edge of the wrapper. Place a heaped teaspoonful of the filling in the middle of a wrapper, then fold in half to form a half-moon shape, pressing the edges together gently. Turn the dumplings so that the seam is on the top, and push down gently on a board or clean work surface to form a flat base on the bottom. Crimp the top seam to seal tightly. Repeat with the remaining dumpling wrappers and filling – you should be able to make about 24.

To cook your potstickers, heat about 1 tablespoon oil in a large non-stick sauté pan (or a frying pan with a lid) over a medium–high heat. Fry half of the dumplings for 2–3 minutes, or until the bases are brown and crisp. Quickly pour 80ml/2½fl oz/5 tablespoons of water into the pan (careful, it may spit) and pop the lid on. Steam for about 5–6 minutes until the venison is cooked and the dough is tender. If they are looking a bit dry during cooking, or if there doesn't seem to be much steam (a glass lid is the best for this), quickly add a little water to the pan – but not too much. All the water should evaporate or be absorbed during this stage of cooking, and the bases of the dumplings should still be crispy. Repeat to cook the other dumplings.

While the dumplings are cooking, mix together the ingredients for the dipping sauce in a small bowl.

Serve the potstickers sprinkled with more sliced spring onions with the dipping sauce alongside.

GREEN GODDESS GUAC

All green, all good. Keeping in with the green theme, perk up your guac with kiwi fruit and wasabi. Serve it with whatever you like your guac with...

2 avocados (about 200g/7oz prepared weight)
2 kiwis, peeled and very finely chopped
grated zest of ½ lime, plus the juice of the whole lime
a handful of fresh coriander/cilantro leaves, finely chopped, plus extra to serve
a good pinch of wasabi powder (or a little wasabi paste), to taste
flaky sea salt

Halve and pit the avocados and use a spoon to scoop the flesh out into a bowl. Using a fork, mash the avocado into a rough purée, leaving it quite chunky. Add the kiwi flesh, lime zest and juice and the chopped coriander and mix in well. Season now with as much wasabi as you dare and plenty of salt.

Serve immediately garnished with a few more coriander leaves.

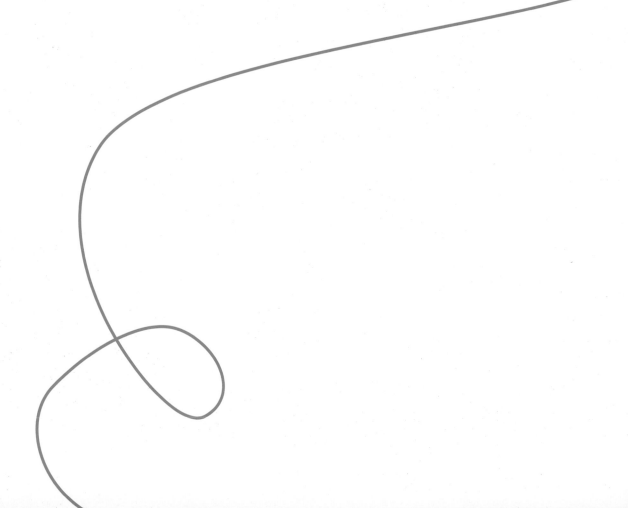

PUNCHY PRAWN AND PEAR SALAD
WITH BLUE CHEESE DRESSING

Pears pair beautifully with blue cheese, but you might not have imagined that prawns/shrimp would work with them both too. Put your inner-sceptic on hold and try this gorgeous salad. I add a touch of Cajun spice to the prawns for a bolder flavour and the whole thing just sings.

2 small, firm but ripe pears

2 small, ripe avocados

300g/10½oz raw, tail-on king prawns/jumbo shrimp

1 corn on the cob

1 tbsp light oil, such as groundnut/peanut

1 tsp Cajun spice

2 little gem lettuces, leaves separated

3 tbsp toasted pumpkin seeds

a few fresh chives, snipped

a few fresh dill fronds

salt

pinch of chilli flakes, to serve (optional)

For the blue cheese dressing:

3 tbsp mayonnaise

3 tbsp soured cream

35g/1¼oz Stilton (or other mild blue cheese), finely crumbled

juice of 1 lemon

sea salt and freshly ground black pepper

Start by making the dressing, so it's ready to go. Combine the mayonnaise, soured cream, blue cheese and most of the lemon juice in a bowl (reserve a little lemon juice for squeezing over the pear and avocado in the next step). Stir everything together, pressing the lumps of cheese against the side of the bowl as you go to break them up and combine it into the sauce. Season generously with salt and pepper and set aside.

Core and halve the pears and chop into slices, keeping all the halves together, cut-sides down on the board, so the slices don't go brown so quickly. Repeat to halve, pit, peel and slice the avocados, again keeping as little of the flesh exposed to the air as possible. Squeeze your reserved lemon juice over the pears and avocados too, which should help prevent browning.

Heat a griddle/grill pan over a high heat. While it's getting really hot, tip the prawns and corn into a bowl, drizzle with the oil, Cajun spice and a generous pinch of salt, and toss them around so that they are coated.

Place the corn on the hot griddle and cook, turning, until charred on all sides. Remove, lay on its side and slice off the kernels. Set aside.

Add the prawns to the griddle and cook for a couple of minutes on each side until pink and cooked through.

To assemble the salad, pile up the lettuce leaves and avocado and pear slices. Add half of the dressing and a sprinkling of salt, and toss well until the leaves are coated. Top with the hot prawns and corn. Finish by sprinkling over the toasted pumpkin seeds and fresh herbs, plus some chilli flakes if you want a little extra heat. Serve the remaining dressing on the side for people to add more to their taste.

HOT LETTUCE TRENCHER
WITH PEAS AND TALEGGIO

This charred warm salad is delightful. Grilling lettuce is a real game changer, if you haven't done it before, creating a wonderful caramelisation and smoky flavour on the outside that contrasts beautifully with the cool, crisp interior. Likewise, charring lemon halves gives them depth and complexity, making them sweeter and less bitter and smoky too. If you can't get Taleggio cheese, you could use fontina, brie or another creamy cheese, but the cheese isn't the main event here and there is only a little; I find Taleggio packs in the right amount of flavour to enhance this gorgeous summery meal.

4 slices sourdough bread

1 large garlic clove, halved

extra virgin olive oil, for drizzling

200g/7oz Taleggio cheese, cut into slices

3 lemons, halved

8–12 asparagus spears (depending on size)

2 heads little gem lettuce

60g/2oz pea shoots

180g/6oz frozen peas, defrosted gently in warm water and drained

For the dressing:

4 tbsp extra virgin olive oil

1 tsp Dijon mustard

a few fresh mint leaves, chopped, plus extra to serve

sea salt and freshly ground black pepper

Heat a ridged griddle/grill pan over a very high heat. Rub the bread slices with the cut side of the garlic, then generously drizzle both sides with olive oil and place on the hot griddle (you may have to do this in batches). Cook for a few minutes until char lines appear on the bread, then remove from the grill and place slices of the Taleggio cheese on each piece of bread to melt a little. Set aside.

Place the lemon halves, cut-sides down, on the griddle. Cook for a few minutes until they are charred, then remove from the griddle.

Drizzle the asparagus spears with a little oil and place on the hot griddle. Cook until tender and char lines appear, turning over halfway through, then remove from the griddle.

Cut the little gem lettuce heads into quarters lengthways so you have eight wedges. Cook four of the wedges, cut-sides down, for a few minutes, making sure not to move them while they are on the griddle so you get strong char lines. Flip them over and cook so that the other cut sides are charred, then remove from the griddle. Repeat to cook the remaining four wedges.

To make the dressing, zest and juice two charred lemon halves into a bowl (set the other lemon halves aside for serving). Add the olive oil and Dijon mustard, and whisk until everything comes together and is emulsified. Taste and season well with salt and pepper. Stir in the mint leaves.

To assemble, place a cheesy charred toast on each plate, followed by a good handful of the pea shoots. Add the charred asparagus and lettuce to the plate. Stir the peas into the dressing then spoon the mixture over the top of everything. Add a sprinkle of salt and pepper, a scattering of small mint leaves and a charred lemon half to each plate, for squeezing.

WATERMELON AND ALFAFA CHAAT

While many Brits may have had a watermelon, mint and feta salad before, this one goes a bit further into Indian *chaat* territory, adding the tangy spice mix chaat masala along with some crunchy gram noodles and nutritious alfalfa sprouts to the refreshing watermelon for a taste sensation.

1kg/2lb 4oz watermelon
40g/1½oz sev noodles (I use thin sev or nylon sev)
80g/3oz salted roasted peanuts, roughly chopped
½–1 green chilli, deseeded and finely chopped
½ red onion, finely chopped
a small bunch of fresh coriander/cilantro,
    roughly chopped
2 tbsp lime juice
2 tsp chaat masala
4 large pinches of alfalfa sprouts (optional)
sea salt

Peel the watermelon and dice the ruby red flesh into 2cm/¾in chunks. Put it in the refrigerator for a few hours to really chill.

Meanwhile, prepare all the other ingredients.

When you are ready to serve, remove the melon from the refrigerator and stir in all the ingredients except the sprouts. Season well with salt and divide among bowls (or tip into one large serving bowl).

Add a large pinch of sprouts (if using) to the top of each bowl and serve.

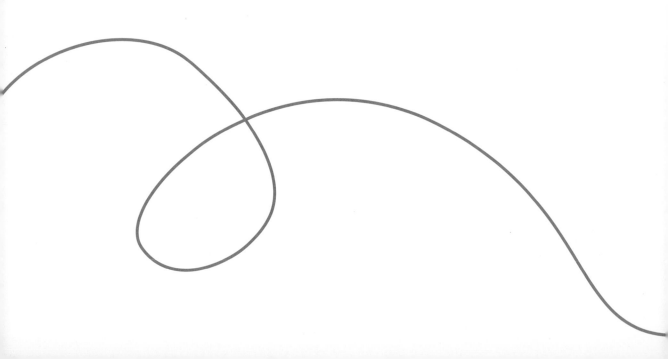

GREEN MANGO AND PISTACHIO CAULIFLOWER STEAKS

Amchoor is a spice not frequently used in Western cuisine – it's probably not something everyone has on their spice rack along with the usual cumin and coriander, but do give it a go if you can find it. This recipe is all about experimenting with new flavours – the sweet-and-sour sharpness the citrussy amchoor brings to this rich starter or light lunch is delightful.

Note: a large cauliflower should easily yield four steaks but you will have leftover cauliflower. See page 96 for a lovely Cauliflower and Dark Chocolate Risotto that will help use up those leftovers.

4 cauliflower steaks, each 2cm/¾in thick
70g/2½oz butter
1 tbsp amchoor
1 tsp ground coriander
1 large garlic clove, crushed
60g/2oz shelled pistachios
1–2 limes, halved
sea salt and freshly ground black pepper

To serve:
1 fresh ripe mango, peeled, stoned and sliced
dollops of thick plain yogurt
a large handful of fresh coriander/cilantro sprigs

Preheat the oven to 220°C/200°C fan/425°F/Gas 7 and line a baking sheet with foil. Lay your cauli steaks on the baking sheet.

Melt the butter in a small bowl in the microwave (or in a small pan on the hob/stovetop) and stir in the amchoor, coriander, garlic and a good pinch of salt. Brush this mixture over both sides of the cauliflower steaks, then bake in the oven for 15 minutes.

Meanwhile, make the pistachio crumb. Finely chop the pistachios, put them in a bowl and season well with salt and pepper.

Once the 15 minutes are up, turn the steaks over. Add the lime halves to the tray and return it to the oven for another 15 minutes, or until the cauli steaks are tender and really starting to take on some colour.

After this time, sprinkle the chopped pistachios over the tops of the cauli steaks and return them to the oven for about 3 minutes to toast the pistachios. Keep an eye on them as they can burn easily.

Serve the cauli steaks with slices of fresh mango, a dollop of yogurt, fresh coriander and a squeeze of the roasted lime juice.

THE MOUNTFIELD BUTTERSCOTCH BRUSSELS

Dare to be different. I'm willing to bet you've never thought of this before, but serving this classic veggie side coated with a spiced butterscotch glaze really works. The sweetness offsets any bitterness in the Brussels and we all know how well bacon takes to the sweet treatment. All credit for this fabulous feast goes to my good friend Andy Mountfield for letting me include his family recipe here. For a lazy version, by all means use a jar of store-bought butterscotch (or sticky toffee) sauce instead of making your own with sugar, butter and cream – just add a few spoonfuls to the hot pan to warm through before you add the Brussels back in. This is great served alongside a roast bird or ham in particular.

500g/1lb 2oz Brussels sprouts, large ones halved
1 tbsp olive oil, plus more if needed
160g/5½oz smoked pancetta lardons
3 echalion shallots, finely sliced into rings
1 red chilli, cut into fine rings
2 tsp chaat masala
30g/1oz/2½ tablespoons soft light brown sugar
25g/¾oz butter
60ml/2fl oz/¼ cup double/heavy cream
a handful of fresh flat-leaf parsley leaves
sea salt

Parboil the sprouts in a large pan of salted, boiling water for 2–3 minutes, or until tender but al dente. Drain and leave to steam dry in the colander.

Meanwhile, heat the oil in a large frying pan and fry the pancetta over a high heat until golden and crispy. Remove from the pan with a slotted spoon, leaving the fat in the pan. Reduce the heat a little and add the shallots. Cook for a few minutes until beginning to caramelise, then stir in the chilli and give that another minute to take off the raw flavour. Remove the shallots and chilli with a slotted spoon, again, leaving any fat in the pan.

Increase the heat to high again, add half the sprouts and sprinkle over 1 teaspoon of the chaat masala. Fry them over a very high heat until they begin to char and caramelise, then tip them into the bowl with the shallots. Repeat with the second half of the sprouts and the remaining 1 teaspoon of chaat masala, adding a little more oil if you need to, cooking until browned again, then removing from the pan.

Reduce the heat to low–medium and add the sugar, butter and cream to the pan. Cook, stirring continuously, for a few minutes until everything is blended and homogeneous and the butterscotch is beginning to thicken.

Tip the shallots, pancetta and sprouts back into the pan with the butterscotch and cook for a minute or so to rewarm everything, stirring the sprouts into the butterscotch glaze to coat them well. Season well with salt and serve with fresh parsley over the top.

BEETROOT PANNACOTTA
WITH CARAWAY AND LEMON CRUMB

MAKES 6

SMALL PLATES

58

There's no need for pannacotta to always be sweet. I sometimes serve this silky, savoury, gorgeously pink pannacotta as a main alongside some pan-fried mackerel. It's essential to add a blob of horseradish sauce to serve (if you are not a fan of horseradish you can also use crème fraîche, which is lovely, but doesn't cut through the richness in the same way). It also goes very well with the Irish Sea Soda Bread on page 61, spread as a sort of pâté, again, with a little horseradish for a bit of pep.

450g/1lb small beetroots/beets
225ml/8fl oz/scant 1 cup whole milk
15g/½oz fresh dill fronds, chopped, plus more picked fronds to serve
5 sheets of leaf gelatine
225ml/8fl oz/scant 1 cup double/heavy cream
½ –1 tsp flaky sea salt
¼ tsp black pepper
creamed horseradish (or crème fraîche), to serve

For the crumbs:
120g/4oz sourdough bread
1 tsp caraway seeds
2 tbsp olive oil
a large pinch of flaky sea salt
finely grated zest of 1 lemon

Preheat the oven to 180°C/160°C fan/350°F/Gas 4. Wrap the beetroots, whole and unpeeled, in a foil parcel, place on a baking sheet and bake for about 1 hour, or until the beetroot is tender all the way through. Leave to cool a little.

Once the beetroots are cool enough to handle comfortably, rub their skins off and dice roughly. Transfer to a food processor with a splash of the milk and blitz to a smoothish purée. Add the rest of the milk and blend again. You may need to use a spatula to keep scraping down the sides of the bowl, but try to get the mixture as smooth as you can – it may take a while. Once the beetroot is smooth, add the dill and pulse a few times to blend in, but don't worry if this still has a bit of texture.

Put the gelatine sheets in a small bowl of cold water to soak until softened, about 5 minutes. Put the cream in a saucepan and heat gently over a low heat until hot but not boiling, then turn off the heat. Squeeze the water out of the gelatine sheets and add them to the cream. Stir until the gelatine has melted and is completely incorporated. Add the beetroot and dill purée and season with the salt and pepper (start with ½ tsp salt and add more to taste). Stir until everything is evenly mixed, then divide the mixture among six silicone pudding moulds or a large muffin tin (each about 130ml/4fl oz/½ cup capacity). Carefully transfer to the refrigerator and leave for a few hours, or ideally overnight, to set completely.

When you are ready to serve, prepare the crumbs. Preheat the oven to 180°C/160°C fan/350°F/Gas 4.

Rip up the bread, put the pieces in a food processor and pulse to coarse crumbs, then transfer them to a bowl. Coarsely grind the caraway seeds in a pestle and mortar and add to the crumbs. Drizzle with the olive oil and add a good pinch of flaky salt, then stir until the oil is well distributed. Tip the crumbs onto a baking sheet and bake for 5 minutes. Give them a stir, then bake for another 5 minutes. Finally, stir in the lemon zest, and give them a final minute in the oven to take off the rawness of the lemon.

Once the pannacottas are fully set, sprinkle a quarter of the crumbs over the centre of each plate. Turn out the pannacottas on top of the crumbs (you may need to dunk the moulds in hot water for a few seconds to loosen them). Finish with a blob of creamed horseradish and a sprinkle of fresh dill fronds, and serve.

IRISH SEA SODA BREAD

The flavours of smoked mackerel and dulse (a dried red seaweed and a favourite Celtic snack) in this moreish soda bread will transport you to the salty, windswept coastlines of the Emerald Isle. It is just perfect served slathered with a horseradish butter (stir 2 tablespoons of prepared horseradish into 125g/4oz softened butter – a tablespoon of chopped fresh chives wouldn't go amiss either – then refrigerate to firm up before using). It also makes a great side to the Beetroot Pannacotta on page 58.

2 smoked mackerel fillets
150g/5oz/1¼ cups plain/all-purpose flour,
   plus extra for dusting
150g/5oz/1 cup wholemeal flour
½ tsp bicarbonate of soda/baking soda
1 tsp baking powder
½ tsp fine sea salt
¼ tsp coarsely ground black pepper
2 tbsp dulse flakes, plus extra to sprinkle
250ml/8½fl oz/1 cup buttermilk
smoked or regular sea salt flakes, to sprinkle
butter, for spreading

Preheat the oven to 200°C/180°C fan/400°F/Gas 6 and line a baking sheet with baking parchment.

Mash the mackerel fillets roughly with a fork until the fish is broken up but still with a fair bit of texture.

Sift the flours, bicarbonate of soda and baking powder into a large bowl and stir in the fine salt, black pepper and dulse flakes. Make a well in the middle of the flour and tip in the buttermilk and the mashed mackerel. Using a fork, stir just to bring the ingredients together to a soft dough. If you overwork it, the bread may be tough.

Lightly flour a work surface and tip the dough onto it. Briefly knead to form the dough into a smooth round ball, then place it on the prepared baking sheet. Sprinkle the top of the dough with smoked or regular sea salt flakes and a little more dulse.

Using a sharp knife, cut a deep cross in the loaf – you want to go at least halfway down to the baking sheet. Bake for about 30 minutes, or until risen and golden and the loaf sounds hollow when tapped on the bottom.

Serve the bread warm from the oven, ripped rustically, with plenty of butter for spreading.

TOMATO ISHTEW

This delicious stew that originally hails from Kerala makes for a substantial and nutritious lunch. I've added some fruity Scotch bonnet chillies to the classic recipe for extra heat.

600g/1lb 5oz (about 8) ripe tomatoes
3 tbsp vegetable oil
1 tsp cumin seeds
1 tsp nigella seeds
2 onions, finely diced
2 celery stalks, roughly chopped
2 carrots, peeled and roughly diced
2 garlic cloves, crushed
2 Scotch bonnet chillies: 1 finely chopped (leave the seeds in for more heat), 1 left whole
1 tsp ground turmeric
1 tsp garam masala
1 x 400g/14oz can coconut milk
200ml/7fl oz/scant 1 cup vegetable stock, or as needed
sea salt, to taste

To serve:
fresh coriander/cilantro
toasted coconut flakes
basmati rice

Bring a pan of water to the boil. Cut out the cores at the top of each tomato and score a small cross in the skin on the bottom of each one. Gently add them to the hot water and blanch for just 15 seconds, then remove with a slotted spoon. As soon as the tomatoes are cool enough to handle, peel away and discard the skins. They should come away easily. Set aside.

Heat the oil in a saucepan over medium–high heat and add the cumin and nigella seeds. Fry until fragrant. Add the onions, then reduce the heat to medium and cook for 10 minutes until golden. Add the celery, carrots, garlic and the chopped chilli, and fry for a good few minutes until softening. Stir in the turmeric and garam masala. Add the whole peeled tomatoes and gently fry for 5 minutes. Add the whole chilli, the coconut milk and enough of the vegetable stock to cover the ingredients. Bring to the boil, then reduce the heat to a simmer and cook for 20 minutes until the vegetables are tender.

Once the vegetables are tender, season the soup to taste. Ladle it into bowls and serve sprinkled with chopped coriander and toasted coconut, with some basmati rice in a bowl on the side for people to add to their stew as they wish.

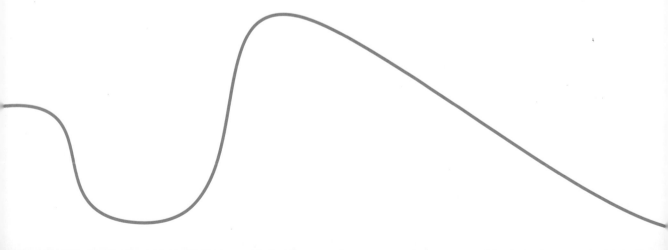

MISO PARMESAN DOUGHNUTS

SAVOURY, SAVOURY, SAVOURY!

These unusual party bites are delicious, blending slightly sweet with savoury and that umami give-me-more effect that miso always has, they will surely be the talking point of your next drinks party. I find this way of rolling out the dough and then stamping it out, scone-style, is much quicker and easier than the conventional way of shaping individual doughnuts. It makes about 12 small doughnuts, ideal for canapés, or 6 large doughnuts if you want to be more indulgent, and you could easily double the recipe if you wanted to.

100ml/3½fl oz/scant ½ cup whole milk
1 tsp caster/superfine sugar
1 x 7g/¼oz sachet fast-action dried yeast
50g/2oz butter
1 large egg, beaten
220g/8oz/1¾ cups strong white bread flour,
   plus extra for dusting
50g/2oz Parmesan cheese, finely grated
½ tsp salt
sunflower oil for deep frying, plus extra for greasing

For the glaze:
25g/¾oz butter
1 tbsp sweet white miso paste
30g/1oz/¼ cup icing/confectioners' sugar

Warm the milk for a few seconds in the microwave until it's lukewarm – don't let it get too hot. Add the sugar and yeast, and stir in, then set aside for a few minutes until the yeast is activated and a froth forms on the top of the mixture.

Meanwhile, melt the butter, then set it aside to cool a little. Once no longer hot, whisk in the egg and the yeast milk mixture.

Sift the flour into a large mixing bowl, or into the bowl of a stand mixer. Add the grated Parmesan and the salt. Make a well in the middle and pour the yeast mixture in. Knead with a dough hook for about 5 minutes until smooth and elastic. If you don't have a stand mixer, stir together with a spoon, then tip out onto a work surface and knead by hand for about 10 minutes. It is quite a soft dough, but that's fine.

Grease a clean bowl with a little oil and pop the dough in. Cover with cling film/plastic wrap and leave to rise in a warm place until doubled in size, about 1–2 hours. Meanwhile, line two baking sheets with non-stick baking parchment.

Once risen, knead the dough briefly to expel the air, then roll out the dough to 2cm/¾in thick. For large doughnuts, use an 8cm/3in round cutter to cut out as many doughnuts as you can. Use a 3cm/1in cutter to cut out the middles, then collect the offcuts, knead together and repeat until the dough is gone – you should get 6 large doughnuts. For small canapé-size doughnuts use a 5cm/2in cutter and a 23mm/¾in cutter for the holes. Transfer the doughnuts to the baking sheets, cover and leave to prove for 1 hour or in the refrigerator overnight.

Fill a large saucepan half-full with oil and heat to 180°C/350°F. Working in batches of 2 or 3 rings at a time, carefully lower each doughnut into the hot oil with a slotted spoon. Fry for about 45 seconds on each side or until golden brown, then remove to drain on paper towels. Repeat until all are cooked, then set aside to cool while you make the glaze.

To make the glaze, melt the butter in the microwave or in a saucepan on the hob/stovetop. Turn off the heat and stir in the miso paste and 1 tablespoon of hot water, then add the icing sugar and stir until everything is well combined. You will need a loose glaze, so add a little more water if you need to.

Once the doughnuts have cooled, dip the tops of the doughnuts in the glaze, then leave them to set on a wire/cooling rack.

FIGGY MEATLOAF

Here the addition of luxurious figs and some Indian spicing lifts the classic meatloaf recipe out of the everyday into more special territory, especially when you dig in to discover the hidden eggs within. It is lovely served as a cold sliced picnic loaf with some fig chutney and salad leaves/greens, but could also work for dinner alongside some mash and seasonal vegetables with a rich gravy.

4 whole eggs

2 tbsp olive oil

1 onion, finely diced

4 garlic cloves, roughly chopped

thumb-sized piece of fresh root ginger, peeled and grated

2 tsp ground cumin

2 tsp ground coriander

a pinch of ground cinnamon

2 tsp garam masala

1 tsp fennel seeds, roughly crushed

16 rashers streaky bacon (about 240g/8½oz total weight)

600g/1lb 5oz minced/ground pork belly

100g/3½oz/1¼ cups fresh breadcrumbs

200g/7oz soft dried figs (snacking figs), roughly chopped

1½ tsp salt

1 egg, beaten

1 tbsp butter, melted

Get a large saucepan of water boiling. Add the whole eggs and boil for 6 minutes. Put the pan under the tap and run cold water over them, then leave them to cool in the pan until completely cool. Once cool, carefully peel off the shells and set aside.

Heat the oil in a frying pan over a medium–high heat and add the onion. Cook for 5 minutes until starting to soften, then add the garlic, ginger and dried spices and cook for a further 5 minutes. Remove from the heat and leave to cool a little.

Meanwhile, preheat the oven to 180°C/160°C fan/350°F/Gas 4. Find yourself a 900g/2lb loaf tin and use 12 of the bacon slices to line the tin, overlapping them slightly and leaving them to overhang the tin at the top.

Put the pork belly in a large bowl and add the breadcrumbs, chopped figs, salt and the spiced onion mixture. Pour in the beaten egg and mix everything together until well combined. Pack about one-third of the mixture into the lined tin, then place the boiled eggs in a row down the centre of the tin, leaving space all around the sides. Pack the remaining meat around the eggs, being careful to keep them in their positions and smooth the top. Fold the overhanging bacon over the top of the meat. Use the remaining bacon slices to cover the top and brush with the melted butter. Cover in foil and bake in the oven for about 45 minutes, then remove the foil and bake for a further 30 minutes, or until cooked through.

Leave the loaf to cool in the tin for a few minutes before turning out to slice and serve. If serving cold, leave it to cool completely in the tin.

'NDUJA
MUSSELS

Add a punch of 'nduja spice to your mussels – they will be out-of-this-world delicious.

1kg/2lb 4oz fresh mussels

25g/¾oz butter

4 echalion shallots, finely sliced

a few fresh thyme sprigs

2 large garlic cloves, finely chopped

80g/3oz 'nduja (from a jar)

3 chargrilled red peppers (from a jar), drained
   and chopped

250ml/9fl oz/1 cup white wine

a small bunch of fresh flat-leaf parsley, chopped

sea salt and freshly ground black pepper

lemon wedges, to serve

crusty bread, to serve

Wash and debeard the mussels. If any are open, give them a few taps with a knife – if they don't close they are probably dead, so discard them.

Heat the butter in a large pot with a lid over a low– medium heat. Add the shallots, thyme and garlic and sauté for a few minutes until the shallots are tender. Add the 'nduja and peppers to the pan and cook for another few minutes until the 'nduja paste has melted down. Add the white wine and the mussels and pop the lid on the pan. Steam for about 5 minutes, shaking the pot halfway through to make sure the mussels cook evenly, until all the mussels have opened – give it a minute or so longer if they haven't. Discard any mussels that are still closed after this time.

Taste the cooking broth and season with salt and pepper (remember the 'nduja will probably be salty, so you may not need much salt), then stir in the parsley. Serve with lemon wedges to squeeze over and chunks of crusty bread to mop up the delicious broth.

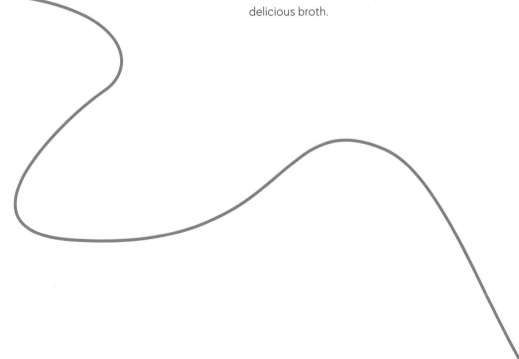

BONE MARROW AND BISCOFF BRIOCHE

Ideal as a roll for a special dinner party or even as a little mid-morning or afternoon snack, this recipe is one for the truly bold, combining bone marrow with the caramelised biscuit spread Biscoff... in a brioche bun! Bone marrow has a wonderful savoury umami flavour, buttery and creamy, and makes a gorgeously rich, silky, surprise filling that you only discover when you bite into these elegant glazed rolls. They need to be served warm from the oven, so bake just before you need them. Spread with butter if serving as a dinner roll, or slathered in a bit more Biscoff for a sweet snack.

Please do make sure to ask a kindly local butcher for the marrow bones. Supermarkets charge a fortune, but your local butcher will probably provide them for just a few quid (and maybe a gift of a few buns in return).

For the filling:

2.4kg/5lb 9oz beef marrow bones
    (about 7 x 10cm/4in lengths)
1½ tsp flaky sea salt, plus a pinch for cooking
    the marrow
90g/3¼oz Lotus Biscoff spread

For the dough:

120ml/4fl oz/½ cup milk
1 x 7g/¼oz sachet fast-action dried yeast
30g/1oz/2 tablespoons caster/superfine sugar
500g/1lb 2oz/4 cups strong white bread flour,
    plus extra for dusting
1½ tsp fine sea salt
4 large eggs, lightly beaten, plus extra beaten
    egg for glazing
150g/5oz butter, at room temperature, cut into
    large dice, plus a little extra for greasing

RECIPE CONTINUES OVERLEAF

To make the filling, preheat the oven to 240°C/220°C fan/450°F/Gas 8 and place the bones, cut-sides up, in a large roasting pan. Sprinkle the tops of the bones with a pinch of flaky sea salt. Bake for about 20 minutes, or until the marrow is just bubbling out; if you insert a skewer into one of the bones, it should go in easily and feel hot to the touch when it's extracted – but don't burn yourself.

Leave the marrow bones to cool down a little in the tray. Once cool enough to handle, extract the marrow by holding each bone over a bowl, inserting a table knife and jiggling it around so the marrow falls into the bowl. Strain it quickly to get rid of most (but not all) of the liquid fat, then tip it back into the bowl, cover and pop it into the refrigerator to cool. (The fat can be used to add flavour to other dishes.)

For the dough, heat the milk in a small bowl for a few seconds in the microwave until just lukewarm. Add the yeast and 1 teaspoon of the sugar and stir together, then set aside for a few minutes until it turns a little frothy.

Meanwhile, sift the flour into the bowl of a stand mixer fitted with a dough hook and add the rest of the sugar and the fine salt to one side. Make a well in the middle and add the beaten eggs along with the yeast and milk mixture. Start the mixer, slowly at first to blend everything together, then keep mixing on medium speed for about 5 minutes until everything is well incorporated and the dough is smooth – it will be quite sticky.

Now start adding the butter, one piece at a time, beating well between each addition. Keep mixing for another minute or so to make sure all the butter is incorporated and the dough is smooth.

Transfer the dough to a clean, greased bowl, cover and leave in a warm place to rise until doubled in size – about 1 hour.

Toward the end of the proving time, finish the filling. Retrieve the chilled bone marrow from the refrigerator and weigh out 175g/6oz. Mix the Biscoff spread into the marrow and add the 1½ teaspoons flaky sea salt. Line two baking sheets with non-stick baking parchment.

Once the dough has doubled in size, divide it into 12 even portions. Dust your hands well and press a portion of the dough out into a large circle in the palm of your hand. Add one-twelfth of the filling to the middle of the circle (about 22g/¾oz) and gather up the edges to make a parcel. Twist the edges to seal, then smooth the bun into a perfect round and place on one of the baking sheets. Repeat to shape the remaining 11 buns, dividing them evenly between the trays and spacing them out so that they have room to expand. Cover the trays with a damp dish towel and leave somewhere warm to rise until doubled in size again – about 1 hour.

Preheat the oven to 220°C/200°C fan/425°F/Gas 7.

Once the buns have proved, brush them all over with the beaten egg (If you LOVE salt, you can also sprinkle the tops with a few more sea salt flakes). Bake the buns for about 13 minutes, or until risen and golden. Leave them to cool for a minute or so, then devour warm.

BIG
PLATES

SIMLA SALMON FISHCAKES

Classic fishcakes but extra. Mild green chillies lend their heat and green beans and coriander lend their fresh green bite to this family favourite. This makes eight generous fishcakes, which could serve four as a main course, or eight as a starter. Serve with a tangle of salad and some mayonnaise or yoghurt raita, with lemon wedges for squeezing.

800g/1lb 12oz white floury potatoes, peeled and cut into large chunks

1 tbsp butter

4 tsp milk, or as needed

1 tbsp vegetable oil, plus extra for shallow frying

1 large red onion, finely diced

a thumb-sized piece of fresh root ginger, peeled and grated

2 x 200g/7oz cans salmon chunks, drained well

75g/2½oz green beans, finely chopped

1 small bunch of fresh coriander/cilantro, finely chopped, plus a few leaves to serve

3 tsp ground coriander

3 tsp ground cumin

2 large mild green chillies, finely chopped

grated zest and juice of 1 lemon

1 tsp salt, or to taste

50g/2oz/scant ½ cup plain/all-purpose flour

2 eggs, lightly beaten

120g/4oz/1¼ cups dried breadcrumbs

Put the potatoes in a large saucepan of water and bring to the boil. Boil for 15–20 minutes, or until tender when you insert a knife. Drain them into a colander and let them steam dry for a couple of minutes. Tip the still warm potatoes back into the pan, add the butter and a little milk, then mash them until smooth, adding only enough milk to get the mixture nice and smooth.

While the potatoes are boiling, cook the onion. Heat the vegetable oil in a frying pan and add the onion. Cook for a good 5 minutes until starting to soften, then add the ginger and cook for a few more minutes until the onion is meltingly soft.

Add the onion and ginger mixture to the mashed potato, along with the drained salmon, green beans, chopped fresh coriander, ground coriander and cumin, chillies, lemon zest and salt. Mix everything together until well combined. Add just half of the lemon juice at first and mix. Depending on the moisture in your can of salmon, you don't want the mixture to get too wet or the cakes will fall apart on cooking – add the rest of the lemon juice only if you think your mixture can take it.

Set up a production line. Put the flour on a plate, the beaten eggs in a shallow bowl and the breadcrumbs onto a second plate. Divide the potato mixture into eight even portions and shape one portion into a patty in the palms of your hands. Dip it first in the flour, then in the beaten egg and finally into the breadcrumbs to fully coat. Repeat to coat the remaining fishcakes.

Heat the oil for shallow frying to a depth of about 1cm/½in in a large frying pan or sauté pan – you want it to come about halfway up the side of the fishcakes. Get it hot and place the fishcakes in the pan – you may have to cook these in batches (and keep them warm in a low oven) depending on the size of your pan. Cook for a few minutes on each side, until golden and piping hot throughout. Serve with accompaniments of your choice, sprinkled with a few more coriander leaves.

WINTER POMEGRANATE PANZANELLA

Panzanella is a popular summertime Italian bread and tomato salad. This autumn/winter version with seasonal vegetables, features jewel-like pomegranates and zesty sumac to provide the acid and aroma that tomatoes usually do. This is not as time-intensive as the recipe length may suggest – there is a bit of baking sheet juggling to do, but it's easy, and the result is packed with flavour.

8 tbsp olive oil

1 tbsp sumac, plus extra to sprinkle

leaves stripped from several sprigs of fresh thyme

2 medium beetroots/beets, peeled, sliced into slim wedges

250g/9oz butternut squash (prepared weight), peeled and cut into large chunks

1 large carrot, peeled and chopped into chunks

2 parsnips, peeled and chopped into chunks

1 red onion, cut into slim wedges

175g/6oz Brussels sprouts

5 garlic cloves, unpeeled

2 tbsp pomegranate molasses

200g/7oz seeded rustic bread or sourdough

5 stems cavolo nero

fresh flat-leaf parsley, roughly chopped, to sprinkle

pomegranate seeds, to sprinkle

sea salt and freshly ground black pepper

For the dressing:
4 tbsp extra virgin olive oil

1 tbsp pomegranate molasses

2 tbsp freshly squeezed orange juice

1 tbsp sherry vinegar

½ tsp Dijon mustard

Preheat the oven to 220°C/200°C fan/425°F/Gas 7. In a small bowl, combine 4 tablespoons of the regular olive oil with the sumac and thyme leaves.

Put the beetroot, squash, carrot and parsnips on a baking sheet. On another sheet, put the onion wedges, sprouts and unpeeled garlic cloves. Drizzle the sumac oil mixture over the vegetables on both sheets, sprinkle generously with salt and pepper, and stir to coat. Put the chunky root veg in the oven first for 25 minutes. After this time, add the second sheet to the oven (move the root veg down and put this on the shelf above). Give both 20 minutes.

Remove both baking sheets from the oven and drizzle the pomegranate molasses over the veg and stir to coat. Return both to the oven (root veg on top this time) and give them a final 5 minutes until everything is golden and caramelised. Tip everything except the garlic into a large bowl and set aside.

Rip the bread into large chunks and place on one of the baking sheets. Rip the cavolo nero into large pieces and place on the other sheet. Drizzle about 3½ tablespoons of the remaining olive oil over the bread and the final ½ tablespoon over the cavolo nero, and mix until well coated. Bake for 5 minutes, then give everything a stir and return to the oven, switching the sheets round. Keep an eye on them after this, checking regularly and removing them from the oven when the bread is golden and toasty and the cavolo nero chips are crispy but still green.

To make the dressing, put all the ingredients in a small bowl and mix together. Remove the papery skins from the roast garlic cloves, mash the flesh and stir that into the dressing too, then season well with salt and pepper.

Add the toasted bread to the bowl with the veg and pour over the dressing. Toss everything well and leave for a few minutes for the bread to soak up all the flavours.

Stir the cavolo nero through the salad just before serving, along with most of the chopped parsley. Transfer to a large bowl, scatter over the remaining parsley and the pomegranate seeds, and serve.

CELERIAC CRUNCH
SALAD

A whole roasted celeriac is a wonderful thing, but it takes many hours in the oven, so I find cooking it sliced into steaks an altogether easier affair. Ideally, the celeriac here should be grilled over charcoal for a smoky flavour, but it can be griddled at a push – the key is to get it properly charred and caramelised and oozing with gorgeous flavour. Paired with hazelnuts in this healthy grain salad, which emphasise the nuttiness of a good celeriac, this makes a substantial lunch dish or elegant supper.

For the celeriac marinade:
1 small celeriac, peeled and cut into 4 'steaks'
3 tbsp olive oil
1 tbsp honey
2 tsp ground cumin
2 tsp ground coriander
1 tsp ground allspice
½ tsp ground cinnamon

For the dressing:
4 tbsp extra virgin olive oil
grated zest and juice of 1 lemon
½ tsp ground cumin
½ tsp ground allspice
1 small garlic clove, crushed
1 tsp honey
sea salt and freshly ground black pepper

For the grain salad:
2 tbsp olive oil
3 echalion shallots, finely sliced
2 x 250g/9oz pouches cooked mixed grains
75g/2½oz blanched hazelnuts, toasted
a small bunch of fresh parsley, roughly chopped

Put the celeriac in a large pan and cover with boiling water. Simmer gently for 10 minutes, then drain and put in a bowl.

Mix together the remaining celeriac marinade ingredients and add to the bowl. Using your hands, gently toss the celeriac until well coated. Leave to marinate for at least 1 hour, or preferably overnight, until you're ready to barbecue or griddle.

Combine all the dressing ingredients and season to taste with salt and pepper.

Prepare the grain salad. Drizzle the oil in a large frying pan, add the shallots and cook over a medium heat until they turn golden and caramelised. Tip into a large bowl, then add the mixed grains to the same pan with a dash of water, stirring occasionally to heat through. Tip the grains into the bowl and immediately add the dressing while still hot. Add most of the toasted hazelnuts and most of the parsley, reserving some for serving. Mix well.

Barbecue or griddle the marinated celeriac on a high heat for 5 minutes on each side until well caramelised and charred.

Roughly chop the celeriac steaks and serve alongside the grain salad with a sprinkling of the reserved hazelnuts and parsley.

GREEK ISLAND TARTE TATIN

Dark, sticky and gorgeous, here I've taken the classic French tarte tatin on holiday to Greece, with unctuous figs and tangy goats' cheese (you could even swap in feta if you wanted). Tarte tatin isn't just a dessert dish, this savoury version makes a delicious light lunch with a lightly dressed tangle of fresh salad leaves/greens.

1 tsp coriander seeds, cracked
75g/2½oz butter
1 tbsp red wine or sherry vinegar
75g/2½oz/⅓ cup caster/superfine sugar
a good pinch of salt
12 figs, halved lengthways
chopped fresh coriander/cilantro, to serve

For the pastry:
75g/2½oz butter, softened
100g/3½oz goats' cheese, crumbled
150g/5oz/1¼ cups plain/all-purpose flour
¼ tsp salt

To make the pastry, beat together the butter and 70g/2½oz of the goats' cheese until well mixed and soft. Sift in the flour and salt, and stir until it all begins to come together, adding the water as you go (you may not need it all). Using your hands, gather the pastry up into a ball and knead briefly on a work surface until smooth. Wrap in cling film/plastic wrap and chill for 30 minutes.

Toward the end of the chilling time, preheat the oven to 210°C/190°C fan/375°F/Gas 6.

Set a heavy 22cm/8½in ovenproof frying pan over a medium heat. Add the coriander seeds to the pan and fry until they become darker in colour and fragrant. Add the butter and let it melt, then stir in the vinegar, sugar and a good pinch of salt, and stir until the sugar has dissolved, then cook to a light caramel.

Arrange the halved figs in the pan, cut-sides down. Let them cook gently over the heat for about 1 minute until softened and beginning to lightly caramelise. While the figs cook, remove the pastry from the refrigerator and roll it out to a circle just larger than the pan. Slide it onto a board and return it to the refrigerator until you are ready to use it.

Working quickly, remove the pastry from the refrigerator and place it over the contents of the pan, tucking the edges down the sides. Transfer the pan to the hot oven and bake for about 25 minutes, or until the pastry is crisp and golden.

Let the tart rest in the pan for a few minutes, then slide a knife around the outside of the pan. Invert a plate on top of the pan and, carefully holding plate and pan together, quickly turn it over to flip the tart out. Sprinkle the remaining goats' cheese over the top and let it melt over the tart and scatter over the fresh coriander. Serve warm.

TEA-SMOKED DUCK SALAD

Home-smoking your own duck is a bold move, but an easy one. And this blend of tea with teriyaki is a perfect blend of two Asian classics. I've chosen Chinese lapsang souchong for its smoky notes without bitterness, which marries beautifully with the Japanese teriyaki sauce on the duck. A lightly dressed noodle and vegetable salad makes a lovely accompaniment. I consider duck rather a treat ingredient, not an everyday one, so I serve this for summer dinner parties when I want something light but impressive.

4 small duck breasts

For the teriyaki marinade:

2 tbsp dark soy sauce

1 tbsp honey

1 tbsp sesame oil

2.5cm/1in chunk of fresh root ginger, peeled and grated

3 large garlic cloves, crushed

4 star anise

For smoking:

15g/½oz/2½ tbsp lapsang souchong loose leaf tea

2 tbsp demerera/turbinado sugar

2 tbsp basmati rice

For the salad dressing:

2 tbsp orange juice

2 tbsp light soy sauce

1 tbsp toasted sesame oil

1½ tbsp rice vinegar

1 tsp honey

1 red chilli, deseeded and finely diced (or leave the seeds in for more heat)

½ tsp finely grated root ginger

For the salad:

140g/4½oz glass/cellophane noodles

1 large carrot, peeled and julienned

1 small red pepper, deseeded and finely sliced

7cm/3in chunk of cucumber, deseeded and julienned

7cm/3in chunk of mooli, peeled and julienned

80g/3oz mangetout/snow peas, finely sliced lengthways

6 spring onions/scallions, shredded

80g/3oz beansprouts

2 tbsp toasted sesame seeds

RECIPE CONTINUES OVERLEAF

First marinate the duck. With a sharp knife, make slashes in the fat across the top of each duck breast, being careful not to cut into the flesh. Combine all the ingredients for the marinade and pour it over the duck breasts in a shallow dish. Turn the duck over in the marinade to make sure all the pieces are well coated, then cover and refrigerate for a few hours. You could do this the day before.

To smoke the duck, line the bottom of a wok (with a lid) with foil and add the tea, sugar and rice. Set a grill (a round cooling rack or splatter screen would work) in the wok, suspended a few inches above the base of the pan. Cover the wok with the lid (or use a piece of strong foil) and place over a medium heat for about 5 minutes, or until it starts smoking. Place the duck breasts on the grill in the wok, re-cover, then turn the heat down to low and leave them to smoke for 8 minutes. Turn the heat off completely and leave everything to cool down in the wok with the lid still on.

Meanwhile, combine all the ingredients for the dressing and set aside.

Cook the noodles according to the package directions, then rinse them well with cold water. Once cool, drain well, then put them in a large bowl with the sliced vegetables and beansprouts.

Once the duck is cool, place the breasts, skin-side down, in a frying pan set over a medium–high heat. Cook for about 4 minutes until the fat renders out of the breasts and they are golden brown underneath. Turn them over with tongs and cook for a further 3 minutes on the other sides, until cooked, but still pink in the middle, tender and juicy. Leave to rest for a few minutes.

While the duck is resting, toss the dressing and most of the sesame seeds through the salad. Transfer to a serving bowl or platter. Slice the duck and serve it on top of the salad, sprinkled with the remaining sesame seeds.

PUTTANESCA CAPER

A perennial favourite of those who like bold flavours, *puttanesca* is already a pretty punchy spaghetti dish, but here I've intensified the flavour even more with some crispy fried capers and fennel seeds. *Buon appetito.*

2 x 50g/2oz cans anchovy fillets in olive oil

3 tbsp extra virgin olive oil, plus a drizzle for the capers

1 tsp fennel seeds

1 tsp dried chilli (hot pepper) flakes

7 garlic cloves, finely sliced

160g/5½oz pitted black olives (the dry, wrinkly ones if possible)

2 x 400g/14oz cans good plum tomatoes in juice (San Marzano, if you can find them)

300g/10½oz dried spaghetti

50g/2oz drained capers

a large handful of fresh parsley leaves, roughly chopped

sea salt and freshly ground black pepper

grated Parmesan cheese, to serve

Pour the olive oil from the anchovy cans into a sauté pan – you should get about 1 tablespoon of oil out of each can. Add the 3 tablespoons olive oil, along with the fennel seeds, chilli flakes, garlic slices and a good pinch of salt. Cook over a gentle heat for about 10 minutes until the garlic is lightly golden and the oil is well infused with the flavours.

Add the anchovies and olives to the pan and stir in, breaking up the anchovies a little with the wooden spoon as you go. Then add the tomatoes and increase the heat to medium–high. Cook for about 15 minutes, stirring frequently, until the sauce is rich, glossy and thickening.

Meanwhile, cook the spaghetti in a large pan of salted water until just tender.

Add a drizzle of olive oil to a frying pan set over a high heat. Pat the drained capers dry with a little paper towel, then add them to the pan. Cook for a couple of minutes until they are beginning to turn brown and you can see them popping. Tip them onto a plate lined with fresh paper towels and pat dry.

Once the pasta and sauce are both cooked, taste the sauce and season with salt and pepper. Transfer the pasta from the water using tongs – don't worry too much if there is still a bit of water on the pasta – this will help loosen the sauce and let it cling to the pasta. Stir the pasta into the sauce until well coated, then stir in the chopped parsley.

Serve the pasta in bowls with the crispy capers sprinkled over the top and plenty of grated Parmesan for people to add to their own bowls.

WILD GARLIC AND NETTLE SPANAKOPITA

Foraged greens in the spring make wonderful and economical alternatives to spinach or garlic in this classic Greek pie. Nettles are nothing to be scared of as long as you wear sturdy gloves when gathering and handling them, but can be subbed for spinach if you're really not keen. Of course, if you're out of season for the wild stuff entirely, the same weight of spinach spiked with a few crushed cloves of regular garlic is traditional and just as delicious.

50g/2oz/⅓ cup pine nuts
150g/5oz butter
100g/3½oz foraged nettles or 200g/7oz fresh
    spinach leaves
200g/7oz foraged wild garlic (leaves and stems;
    save any flowers for garnish)
1 tbsp olive oil
1 large banana shallot, finely chopped
½ tsp ground allspice
a large handful of fresh dill, roughly chopped
2 large eggs, beaten
200g/7oz feta cheese, crumbled
6 large sheets filo/phyllo pastry
sesame seeds, to sprinkle
sea salt and freshly ground black pepper

Preheat the oven to 200°C/180°C fan/400°F/Gas 6 and line a baking sheet with baking parchment. While you're preheating the oven, toast the pine nuts on a separate baking sheet for a few minutes until golden and toasty, then leave them to cool.

Melt 25g/1oz of the butter in a large sauté pan over a low heat. Wash the nettles/spinach and wild garlic well and give them a quick shake – it doesn't matter if there's still water clinging to the leaves. Put them in the pan with the butter, pop the lid on and let them wilt down for a few minutes, stirring occasionally. Once wilted, transfer to a plate lined with paper towels and leave to cool and steam dry a little more.

Melt another 25g/1oz of butter with the oil in the same pan and add the shallot and allspice. Cook for a few minutes until softened, then stir in the dill and turn the heat off.

Pat the wilted leaves with paper towels, pressing down to remove as much liquid as you can, then roughly chop them and add to the pan. Stir in the toasted pine nuts, egg and feta cheese, and season with plenty of pepper and a little salt (remembering that the feta is salty).

Clear a large space on your work surface and lay out three sheets of the filo pastry, short end to end, overlapping each by 3cm/1in. Melt the remaining butter and brush the sheets generously with it using a pastry brush. Repeat to add another layer of filo using three more of the sheets, then brush them with butter too.

By this point, your filling should be almost cool. Spoon it, in a long line, onto one long side of the filo, going the whole way along, about 3cm/1in in from the edge. Roll up the filo, encasing the filling, so you have a long sausage. Roll that sausage into a tight spiral, then transfer it carefully to the prepared baking sheet. Brush liberally all over with remaining melted butter and sprinkle with sesame seeds.

Bake the spanakopita for about 45 minutes, until the pastry is golden and the filling piping hot. Serve warm, scattered with wild garlic flowers if you have them.

HALLOUMI
SALTADO

Lomo saltado is a traditional Peruvian dish of seared marinated sirloin with punchy stir-fried veg and fries. It's magnificent when done well and normally calls for Peruvian ají Amarillo paste, but you can use ancho for this, or whatever chilli paste is easily available. It's a versatile recipe, so I've swapped in halloumi for the steak for a vegetarian version, the firmness of which gives the right texture and it can be oven-baked along with the fries; ideal for family dinnertime.

500g/1lb 2oz frozen oven fries
500g/1lb 2oz halloumi cheese (2 packs)
2 tbsp olive oil, plus extra for the halloumi
4 tbsp soy sauce
1½ tbsp red wine vinegar
1 tbsp runny honey
2 tsp ground cumin
1 tsp dried oregano
2 tsp chilli paste of choice
1 red onion, finely sliced
1 red pepper, deseeded and chopped into chunks
1 green pepper, deseeded and chopped into chunks
2 fresh tomatoes, deseeded and sliced
a small bunch of fresh coriander/cilantro, roughly chopped
1 red chilli, finely sliced, to garnish (optional, for those who like more heat)
sea salt and freshly ground black pepper

Preheat the oven to 220°C/200°C fan/425°F/Gas 7.

Cook the oven fries according to the package directions.

Slice the halloumi into strips lengthways and brush them generously with oil. After about 15 minutes of the fries cooking, give them a stir and add the halloumi to the baking sheet. Cook them together for another 10 minutes or so, turning the halloumi over halfway through, until both the fries and cheese are golden.

Meanwhile, add the soy sauce, vinegar, honey, cumin, oregano, chilli paste and a pinch of salt and pepper to a small bowl and mix to combine well.

Heat the 2 tablespoons of oil in a wok over a medium–high heat. Add the red onion and let it start to soften for a couple of minutes. Add the peppers and cook for a couple more minutes until the onion is soft and the peppers are taking on some colour, then add the tomatoes and your soy mixture. Cook for another couple of minutes, until the tomatoes are softening and the peppers are tender.

As soon as the fries and halloumi come out of the hot oven, quickly stir them into the stir-fry along with most of the coriander. Serve immediately sprinkled with the remaining coriander and the red chilli, if using.

CASHEW AND MUSHROOM STROGANOFF

This is a refreshing and light vegan take on a stroganoff, which can sometimes be a bit claggy and heavy. It makes a perfect weeknight dinner for all the family. For a real gourmet feast, look out for wild mushrooms when they hit the supermarket or greengrocers in season – they will add so much more flavour and savoury umami to this already lovely dish.

200g/7oz cashew nuts

3 tbsp sunflower or vegetable oil

500g/1lb 2oz mixed mushrooms, roughly sliced or just halved if small

1 onion, finely sliced

2 large garlic cloves, crushed

1 tbsp wholegrain mustard

200ml/7fl oz/scant 1 cup vegetable stock

a large handful of fresh mint leaves, roughly chopped, plus extra small leaves to serve

salt and freshly ground black pepper

cooked pappardelle or tagliatelle pasta (check that it is vegan, if necessary), to serve

First, make the cashew cream. Put 120g/4oz of the cashews in a heatproof bowl and pour over enough boiling water from the kettle to cover. Leave to soak for about 30 minutes, then drain them. Put them in a high-speed blender with 200ml/7fl oz/scant 1 cup fresh water and blend until smooth.

While your cashews are soaking, preheat the oven to 200°C/180°C fan/400°F/Gas 6, then toast the remaining cashews for 5 minutes, or until golden brown. Leave to cool, then finely chop half of them.

Heat 1 tablespoon of the oil in a large sauté pan over a high heat. Add half the mushrooms and cook them quickly and intensely until browned and wilted. Remove them from the pan and repeat with another 1 tablespoon of oil and the remaining mushrooms. Once cooked, remove all the mushrooms from the pan and set aside on a plate.

Reduce the heat to low–medium and add the remaining oil to the pan with the onion. Cook gently for a good 8–10 minutes until the onion is soft and translucent, then add the garlic and give it a couple more minutes. Stir in the mustard, then return the mushrooms to the pan, add the stock and simmer for a few minutes until the liquid is reduced by half.

Add the cashew cream and mint to the pan along with the toasted cashews (keep the chopped ones to one side). Cook until the liquid is warmed through again and you have a homogeneous creamy sauce. Add a splash more water if the sauce is too thick. Taste and season well with salt and pepper.

Serve the stroganoff immediately over cooked pasta, with the chopped toasted cashews and a few more mint leaves sprinkled over the top.

CAULIFLOWER AND DARK CHOCOLATE RISOTTO

This smoothly savoury risotto has a surprising addition in the form of grated dark chocolate. It might sound a little strange but the bittersweet fruity tones of good dark chocolate enhance and boost the nuttiness of the fresh cauliflower, adding richness and complexity. I also love the contrast and drama of the almost black chocolate strewn across the creamy white risotto on the plate.

30g/1oz butter

1 tbsp olive oil

1 large onion, finely diced

2 celery stalks, finely diced

2 large garlic cloves, crushed

260g/9½oz risotto rice (such as arborio or carnaroli)

185ml/6fl oz/¾ cup white wine (about 1 mini bottle)

750ml/25fl oz/3 cups hot vegetable stock (strained if you'd like to keep the risotto as creamy white as possible)

250g/9oz cauliflower, chopped into small florets

50g/2oz Parmesan cheese, finely grated

60ml/2fl oz/¼ cup double/heavy cream

about 40g/1½oz dark/bittersweet chocolate (85% cocoa solids), or more to taste

sea salt and white pepper

Melt the butter with the oil in a large saucepan over a low–medium heat and add the onion and celery. Cook for 8–10 minutes until tender and translucent, but not colouring. Add the garlic and cook for another couple of minutes.

Add the risotto rice to the pan and stir it around for a minute to get it well coated in the flavoured butter. Pour in the wine and let it cook down until almost all the liquid has gone. At this point, start adding the hot stock a little at a time, allowing the latest addition to be absorbed before adding the next, stirring very regularly.

After about 10 minutes of adding stock and stirring, add the cauliflower and continue the same process for another 10 minutes or so, until all the stock is incorporated and both the cauliflower and rice are just slightly al dente. The risotto should be thick but still loose – the consistency of rolling lava.

Turn off the heat, stir in the Parmesan and cream, and beat vigorously until everything is well incorporated. Put a lid on the pan and leave to rest for a few minutes while you grate the chocolate and pop it into a small bowl.

Once the risotto has rested, taste and season well with salt and white pepper, then serve immediately with the grated chocolate spooned generously over the top.

VEGGIE APRICOT BUNNY CHOW

Rabbit food this is NOT. This flavoursome curry, studded with juicy dried apricots, is an Indian South African dish, usually served in a hollowed-out loaf, which acts as a portable container for the curry. It's a favourite on the streets of Durban and is truly substantial – a meal that will keep you going all day. Eat as a sharing meal with your hands, tearing off chunks of bread to scoop up the sauce for the most authentic experience. The gravy-soaked bit at the end is the ultimate treat for those who persevere.

3 tbsp olive oil
1 large white onion, finely diced
5cm/2in piece of fresh root ginger, peeled and grated
2 large garlic cloves, grated
2–3 red chillies, finely chopped (deseed for less heat)
1 tbsp garam masala
2 tsp ground cumin
1 tsp ground coriander
1 tsp ground turmeric
½ tsp ground cinnamon
5 dried curry leaves
1 x 400g/14oz can chopped tomatoes
1 large carrot, peeled and diced
300g/10½oz sweet potato, peeled and diced
300g/10½oz cauliflower florets
1 yellow, orange or red pepper, deseeded and diced
100g/3½oz soft dried apricots, halved
2 tbsp apricot jam
2 round, crusty loaves of bread
a bunch of fresh coriander/cilantro, roughly chopped, plus a few sprigs to serve
a good squeeze of lemon juice
sea salt and freshly ground black pepper

For the minty yogurt:
6 tbsp thick Greek yogurt
a small handful of fresh mint leaves, shredded
a squeeze of lemon juice

Heat the oil in a large saucepan set over a low–medium heat and cook the onion for about 6 minutes until really soft. Add the ginger, garlic, red chillies, dried spices and curry leaves, and cook for another 3–4 minutes. Add the chopped tomatoes and swill out the can with another 300ml/10½fl oz/1¼ cups or so of water and add that too. Tip in the carrot and sweet potato and give everything a stir. Increase the heat to medium and bring to the boil, then pop the lid on the pan and cook for 20 minutes until the veg are beginning to soften.

After this time, add the cauliflower florets, pepper and apricots, and stir in the apricot jam. Cook for another 15 minutes, or until all the vegetables are tender, stirring occasionally and adding a little more water if you think it is getting too thick or beginning to catch on the base of the pan.

Meanwhile, slice the top off each loaf of bread and hollow out the middles (see tip, below).

Combine all the ingredients for the minty yogurt in a small bowl and season with a little salt and pepper.

Once the curry is cooked, stir in the chopped coriander and lemon juice, then taste and season with salt and pepper. Ladle the curry into the loaves and finish with a blob of minty yogurt and a few coriander sprigs on top. Serve one loaf per two people and dig in.

Tip: Keep the leftover insides of the loaves to blitz for breadcrumbs to store in the freezer.

CHILLI CRAB
MAC 'N' CHEESE

I've ramped up the often bland flavour of mac 'n' cheese here with the bold punchy flavours of Korean chilli crab. Gochujang is a sweet and spicy fermented condiment, which is quite easy to find in supermarkets now. The dish is quite rich, so do serve it with a salad of peppery leaves and tomatoes and maybe a side of kimchee for a balancing sharpness.

400g/14oz dried macaroni
50g/2oz butter
50g/2oz/scant ½ cup plain/all-purpose flour
550ml/19fl oz/2¼ cups whole milk
1½ tbsp gochujang (Korean chilli paste),
  or more to taste
200g/7oz Cheddar cheese, grated
3 x 110g/3¾oz cans lump crabmeat, drained
4 jarred chargrilled peppers, sliced (optional)
40g/1½oz/½ cup fresh breadcrumbs
finely shredded spring onions/scallions and red chilli,
  to sprinkle
sea salt
salad and kimchee, to serve

Bring a large pan of water to the boil and add a good pinch of salt. Add the macaroni and cook according to the package directions until tender.

Meanwhile, melt the butter in another large saucepan and add the flour. Cook over a low heat for a few minutes to cook out the flavour of the flour. Slowly start adding the milk, a little at a time, whisking between additions to get rid of any lumps. Once all the milk is added, cook for about 5 minutes over a medium heat, stirring very frequently, until the sauce has thickened. Stir in the gochujang and most of the cheese, reserving a handful for the top.

Preheat the grill/broiler to medium–high. Once the pasta has cooked, drain it in a colander and tip it into the pan with the sauce. Stir so that it is well coated, then tip in the crabmeat and peppers, if using, and fold in. Taste to check the seasoning and add salt – or more gochujang, if you want it spicier – to taste.

Tip the macaroni and cheese into a large baking dish and sprinkle the top with the reserved cheese and breadcrumbs. Place the dish under the grill for a few minutes until the top is golden and the breadcrumbs crisp. Sprinkle the top with the shredded spring onion and chilli curls (see tip, below), and serve with a salad and kimchee for balance.

Tip: For beautiful spring onion and chilli curls to top your masterpiece, very finely shred them, then pop into a bowl of iced water. They will curl up elegantly. Pat dry on paper towels before using to top your dish.

THAI TEQUILA TROUT

One of my favourite supper dishes is my Gin and Tonic Salmon, which matches herbs and botanicals with the delicate flavours of the fish. It set me thinking about other herbal combinations to complement fish and in a flash of inspiration, I realised that the pungently aromatic herbs of Thailand – galangal, makrut (kaffir) lime, lemongrass – might be the perfect foil for the oily flesh of trout. My penchant for alliteration pushed me to see whether tequila rather than gin might be the spirit of choice in this case and it worked beautifully. An elegant dish for a summer's evening. A tequila soda and lime on the side is entirely optional, but advised.

4 whole rainbow trout, gutted and cleaned
250ml/9fl oz/1 cup soda water
sea salt and freshly ground black pepper

For the marinade:
4 tbsp tequila
finely grated zest and juice of 1 lime
3 garlic cloves, crushed
a small chunk of galangal, peeled and grated
1 lemongrass stalk, finely shredded
6 makrut (kaffir) lime leaves, finely shredded
½ red chilli, finely diced
1 tsp ground coriander

To serve:
a handful of fresh coriander/cilantro
flaky sea salt
lime wedges
cooked rice

The night before you want to cook the dish, marinate the fish. Put all the marinade ingredients in a small bowl and season with salt and pepper. Spread a quarter of the mixture inside each trout, then put the trout in a large baking dish and pour over the soda water. Place in the refrigerator overnight.

The next day, remove the fish from the refrigerator and preheat the oven to 200°C/180°C fan/400°F/ Gas 6. Place the dish in the oven and bake for about 20 minutes, or until the fish is opaque and cooked through.

If the sauce has not reduced sufficiently, remove the fish to a plate and cover with foil to keep warm. Tip all the juices from the pan into a saucepan and place over a medium heat. Let the liquid bubble over the heat until it has reduced to a sticky sauce.

Serve the trout with the sauce poured over the top and a scattering of fresh coriander leaves. Sprinkle with flaky salt and provide limes on the side, as is obligatory with your tequila. Serve with rice.

COD AND POPCORN GRATIN

Lift a family-style gratin out of the everyday and into extraordinary territory with the addition of wasabi, for some fresh clean heat. For an added level of excitement, I have played on the corn flavours here and added some buttery toasty popcorn on top. Ideally it needs to be eaten on the day it is made, as the popcorn topping does go soggy in the refrigerator, although it still tastes nice. For an easy life, use a bag of shop-bought salted popcorn if you don't want the extra step of popping your own.

For the topping:

2 tbsp vegetable or sunflower oil
50g/2oz/¼ cup popcorn kernels
50g/2oz salted butter, melted
sea salt flakes

For the filling:

40g/1½oz butter
1 large leek (or 2 smaller), finely sliced
kernels sliced from 2 corn cobs (or 200g/7oz drained canned sweetcorn or thawed frozen sweetcorn)
3 tbsp plain/all-purpose flour
350ml/12fl oz/generous 1⅓ cups whole milk, plus extra if needed
80g/3oz Cheddar cheese, grated
100g/3½oz baby spinach leaves
550g/1lb 3oz cod fillets, chopped into large chunks
about 1 tbsp wasabi powder (or paste), or more to taste
a large handful of fresh parsley leaves, chopped
2 tbsp lemon juice
sea salt and freshly ground black pepper

First make the topping, so it's ready to go. Heat the oil in a large saucepan with a lid over a medium heat. Add the popcorn kernels and put the lid on the pan. After a few seconds you will begin to hear popping. Keep the pan over the heat, giving it a shake occasionally, until the popping really slows down, then turn off the heat. Tip the popped corn into a food processor, being careful to leave behind any hard, unpopped kernels, and pulse to a coarse crumb. Tip the crumbs into a bowl, pour in the melted butter and a good pinch of sea salt flakes, and stir so the corn is well coated in the butter. Set aside.

For the filling, heat the butter in a large saucepan over a low–medium heat, add the leek and sauté for a few minutes until softened. Add the corn and cook for a minute or so before sprinkling the flour over the top and stirring in. Pour in the milk and cook gently for about 5 minutes until the sauce is thickening.

Meanwhile, preheat the grill/broiler.

Add two-thirds of the Cheddar to the pan and stir in until melted, then stir in the spinach and the cod – be gentle with the cod as you don't want to break it all up. Cook for another couple of minutes until the spinach is wilted into the sauce and the cod is almost cooked. Stir in the wasabi, parsley and lemon juice, then taste and season well with salt and pepper. Add a splash more milk if the filling is a little thick.

Tip the filling into a baking dish and sprinkle the buttery popcorn over the top. Scatter the remaining cheese over the top and place the dish under the grill for a few minutes until the popcorn is golden and toasted and the cheese is melted. Serve immediately, otherwise the popcorn has a tendency to go soggy if left too long.

THAT CHICKEN T'ING

Nothing if not eclectic, this is a twist on an American Southern States classic: beer-can chicken, taking a hop over the border into Mexico for the spice rub and a boat over the sea to Jamaica for the fizz. I've cooked it in the oven for ease, but it works perfectly over a barbecue in the summer months, for a really authentic smoky finish. Ting is a Jamaican grapefruit-flavoured soda – both tart and sweet, it lends a subtle fruity flavour to the meat while still retaining that slightly bitter edge that beer would bring. And that Mexican spice rub on the chicken skin, which crisps up gloriously due to the upright cooking method, means it's great served in Mexican-style tacos with lots of pretty salads, piquant salsas and seasonings of your choice, but would be equally good with a fresh slaw and some potato wedges.

1 tbsp olive oil

1.5kg/3lb 5oz chicken

1 lemon, halved

1 x 330ml/11fl oz can Ting soda (or limeade works well too)

For the Mexican spice rub:

1 tsp onion powder

1 tsp garlic powder

1 tsp dried thyme

2 tsp smoked paprika

2 tsp ground cumin

2½ tsp chipotle chilli flakes

2 tsp sea salt

½ tsp ground black pepper

¼ tsp ground cinnamon

a pinch of ground cloves

Preheat the oven to 220°C/200°C fan/425°F/Gas 7 and rearrange your oven shelves so you have plenty of space height-wise.

In a small bowl, combine all your spices for the Mexican rub.

Rub the oil all over the chicken and squeeze over the juice of one of your lemon halves. Next, sprinkle over your Mexican rub. Make sure the chicken is well coated with all the flavourings.

Pour out half the can of soda (you can drink this), then sit the can with its remaining soda in a deep roasting pan. Add the remaining lemon half to the cavity of the chicken, then firmly push the chicken onto the soda can, so the can sits inside the cavity and the chicken is standing up. Make sure it's secure and won't fall over.

Transfer the chicken to the oven and roast for about 1 hour 15 minutes, turning the oven down to 180°C/160°C fan/350°F/Gas 4 after the first 30 minutes. Baste several times during cooking, and when the time is up, check that the chicken is cooked through – the juices should run clear when the thickest part of the thigh is pierced with a skewer. Carefully remove the chicken from the can and leave to rest for a few minutes before carving and serving.

CRUNCHY-NUT CHICKEN BURGERS

WITH SPICY MAYO

This intriguing mash-up takes the humble chicken burger to Indonesia by way of everyone's favourite peanutty breakfast cereal. Weird maybe, wonderful definitely. The first time I made this I was still trying to decide whether it worked when I finished the whole thing in about three minutes flat, so I guess it did.

I took the inspiration from *gado gado* salad and made a kecap manis (Indonesian sweet soy sauce) mayo to go with it, along with chillies and ginger to stop it getting overly sweet. This is also balanced out with a salad of sharp radish and pickles, and fresh cucumber. It is everything you want in a meal – sweet, salty, sour, spicy, nutty, crunchy, soft, crisp, juicy – utterly compelling.

4 skinless boneless chicken breasts
300ml/10½fl oz/1¼ cups buttermilk
100g/3½oz/generous ¾ cup plain/all-purpose flour
2 tsp garlic granules
2 tsp mild chilli powder
2 eggs, beaten
200g/7oz honey nut cornflakes
   (such as Kellogg's Crunchy Nut)
neutral oil, for frying
sea salt and freshly ground black pepper

For the pickles:
4–6 radishes, finely sliced
2 tbsp rice vinegar
1 tsp honey
a pinch of salt

For the kecap mayo:
4 tbsp mayo
2 tbsp kecap manis
1 tbsp peanut butter
1–2 tbsp fresh lemon juice
¼ red chilli, deseeded and finely diced
5mm/¼in piece of fresh root ginger, peeled and grated
sea salt

To serve:
4 brioche burger buns
lettuce leaves
cucumber

RECIPE CONTINUES OVERLEAF

Slice each chicken breast into three or four thick strips – we are going for maximum crispy coverage here, which will be better achieved with more pieces than a whole breast. Put them in a bowl and add the buttermilk along with a pinch of salt and pepper. Leave to marinate for a few hours in the refrigerator to tenderise the chicken, but let it come to room temperature for 20 minutes before coating and cooking.

To make the pickles, put the radishes in a small bowl with the rice vinegar and 1 tablespoon water. Add the honey and salt, stir together, then leave to pickle for at least 30 minutes – or a few hours (in the refrigerator) if you want them to go completely pink, which looks great.

For the kecap mayo, combine all the ingredients in a small bowl, adding more lemon juice and salt to taste.

Once the chicken has marinated, set up a production line. Put the flour on a plate, mix in the garlic and chilli powder, and season well with salt and pepper. Put the beaten eggs in a shallow bowl. Crush the cornflakes into smaller pieces, but not completely to crumbs, and put them on another plate. Remove a piece of chicken from the buttermilk and shake it to remove any excess liquid. Dip it first in the flour, then in the egg and finally in the cornflake crumbs, making sure it is completely covered at every step. Repeat to coat all of the chicken pieces.

Heat a 1.5cm/⅔in depth of oil in a sauté pan or deep frying pan over a medium heat. Once hot, fry the chicken pieces for a couple of minutes on each side until golden and crispy and cooked through. You will probably need to cook them in batches. Drain the pieces on paper towels while you cook the next batch.

To assemble your burgers, halve the brioche buns and lightly toast the cut sides on a hot dry griddle/grill pan or frying pan. Spread the base of the buns with a little of the kecap mayo, then layer up with lettuce leaves, cucumber slices, pickles and chicken pieces. Drizzle a little more mayo over the chicken, then pop the lids on the buns and enjoy.

CASSOULET DE FULL ENGLISH

This fusion of a British classic cooked in a French style mixes things up a bit. The highly seasoned black pudding breaks down and forms the base of a flavoursome stock for a delicious, substantial, beany supper dish. I used canned haricot/navy beans for ease, but you could also soak 250g/9oz dried beans in plenty of water overnight, then drain and add to the pan at the same time as the tomatoes, cooking for about 2 hours, stirring every 30 minutes, until tender.

2 tbsp olive oil, plus extra if needed

8 good pork sausages

6 slices smoked streaky bacon, roughly chopped

2 thick slices black pudding (about 115g/3¾oz)

130g/4oz chestnut/cremini mushrooms, roughly diced

1 large onion, finely diced

2 celery stalks, finely diced

2 medium carrots, peeled and finely diced

2 large garlic cloves, finely chopped

leaves from a few sprigs of fresh thyme

1 x 400g/14oz can chopped tomatoes

2 x 400g/14oz cans dried haricot/navy beans, drained and rinsed

3 tbsp tomato ketchup, plus extra to serve

4 small slices of sourdough bread

butter, for spreading

4 eggs

sea salt and freshly ground black pepper

RECIPE CONTINUES OVERLEAF

Preheat the oven to 180°C/160°C fan/350°F/Gas 4.

Heat the oil in a large casserole dish over a high heat. Brown the sausages on all sides, then remove them from the pan and set aside.

Add the chopped bacon to the same pan and cook until it is golden and crispy, then turn the heat down to medium. Add the mushrooms to the pan (with another drizzle of oil if you need to) and cook for a couple of minutes until beginning to brown, then add the black pudding. Cook for a few minutes more until the mushrooms are browned and wilted, and the black pudding is beginning to break down, then add the onion, celery, carrots, garlic and thyme. Cook more gently now for about 7–8 minutes until the veg is softening.

Tip in the canned tomatoes then swill out the can with another generous can full of water (about 500ml/17fl oz/2 cups) and add that, too. Add the sausages back to the pan along with the haricot beans and stir everything together. Put the lid on the pan, place in the preheated oven and cook for 1 hour 15 minutes–1 hour 30 minutes, giving it a stir every 30 minutes or so, or until everything is cooked through. After this time, stir the ketchup into the cassoulet, then taste and adjust the seasoning – you probably won't need that much salt and pepper as the black pudding is highly seasoned.

Toast your slices of bread, then spread them with butter. Place them on top of the cassoulet and crack an egg onto the top of each slice. Cover the pan with a lid again and cook for 5–6 minutes until the egg whites are set but the yolks are still runny. Alternatively, you can cook your eggs to your liking in a separate frying pan and simply top the toast slices with them when done. Season with a sprinkle of black pepper.

Serve the cassoulet in the pan with extra ketchup on the side.

CHICKEN AND BANANA KORMA

My easy chicken korma is a classic recipe that I make time and again, full of comforting creaminess and gentle warming spice, but it's not what I would call bold. So, I ask you this – what about adding an ingredient you might never have thought would work in a savoury dish – banana. *Banana?* I hear you cry. Yes, banana! It brings a sweet nuttiness to the sauce and a gentle fruitiness that complements the spicing. It also means that you can use less refined sugar to get the familiar sweetness that so defines this family favourite. Try it – you won't be disappointed.

100ml/3½fl oz/scant ½ cup vegetable oil

2 onions, diced

4 garlic cloves, crushed

2 thumb-sized pieces of fresh root ginger, peeled and grated

2 tbsp garam masala

¼ tsp chilli powder

1 tsp ground turmeric

1½ tsp salt

600g/1lb 5oz chicken (breasts or thighs), diced

2 bananas, peeled and chopped into thick slices

100g/3½oz creamed coconut

200ml/7fl oz/scant 1 cup crème fraîche

3 tbsp ground almonds

1 tbsp sugar (any type)

fresh coriander/cilantro, to sprinkle

cooked rice, to serve

Heat the oil in a large frying pan over a medium heat and add the onions. Cook for 6–7 minutes, stirring frequently, until they are beginning to soften and caramelise. Add the garlic and ginger and cook for a couple of minutes more.

Add the dried spices and salt to the pan, followed by the chicken pieces. Cook for a few minutes, again stirring frequently, until the chicken is browned all over.

Pour 300ml/10½fl oz/1¼ cups water into the pan and stir everything together. Bring the liquid to a lively simmer and cook, uncovered, for about 10 minutes. Add the bananas and cook for another 2–3 minutes until the chicken is cooked through and the sauce has thickened.

Reduce the heat to low and stir in the creamed coconut, crème fraîche, ground almonds and sugar. Try to be careful when you stir so that you don't break up the banana, which may get soft. Cook for a minute just to warm the crème fraîche through, then serve straight away with cooked rice, sprinkled with fresh coriander.

AMARETTO LAMB RAAN

The traditional way of cooking large joints of meat in India (before the advent of domestic ovens) would be in an underground pit or in a commercial tandoor oven; a time-consuming method of cooking and therefore definitely reserved for special occasions. A *raan* then is a deeply flavoursome juicy roast cooked in a warming cloak of spiced paste that is ideal for a Sunday dinner or for a celebration feast. Inspired by one of my favourite inventions, gingerbread *raan*, I wondered what other sweet flavours could work in the same way to create a sticky, toothsome marinating glaze, and amaretto – the sweet, syrupy Italian almond liqueur that also lends its aromatic punch to crunchy biscuits – fitted the bill. This works as well with Indian accompaniments, such as raita, naan or rice and some lime wedges, as it does with roast potatoes and some spring vegetable sides, or even some crispy-skinned jacket potatoes.

2 white onions, roughly chopped
4cm/1½in piece of fresh root ginger
6 garlic cloves, peeled
2 tsp garam masala
2 tsp ground cinnamon
1 heaped tsp ground cumin
2 heaped tsp ground coriander
1 tbsp lightly crushed fennel seeds
3 tbsp soft light brown sugar
2 tbsp flaky sea salt
450g/1lb amaretto biscuits
3 tbsp amaretto liqueur
3 tbsp vegetable oil
2kg/4lb 8oz leg of lamb
charred lime halves, to serve

Preheat the oven to 170°C/150°C fan/325°F/Gas 3.

Put the onions, ginger, garlic, spices, sugar, salt, amaretto biscuits, liqueur and oil into a food processor and blitz to a thick paste.

Use a sharp knife to make deep insertions in the meat over the thickest part of the lamb leg. Pour the amaretto paste over the leg and spread it around with your hands, making sure you get lots into the slashes to let more flavour in.

Transfer the lamb to a large roasting pan and pour in 250ml/9fl oz/1 cup water. Cover the pan with foil (try to create a tent over it so the foil doesn't stick to the paste and scrape it off the lamb). Roast in the oven for 2½ hours until the lamb is tender, then remove the foil, turn the heat up to 220°C/200°C fan/425°F/Gas 7 and give it a last 20 minutes at the higher heat to brown it a little.

Remove from the oven and let it rest a little before serving with some charred lime halves for squeezing.

JAMAICAN JERK PORK
WITH PINEAPPLE SLAW

Big flavours, with a real spice kick, the soft brown sugar in the seasoning rub helps to permeate the skin of the pork as it marinades and also adds a lovely stickiness. This would also be fantastic barbecued to really boost those smoky flavours. A homemade pineapple slaw is the perfect complement here.

1.5kg/3lb 5oz pork belly (you need one as even in depth as possible, for even cooking)
a little olive oil, for drizzling
1 tsp sea salt flakes

For the Jamaican jerk rub:
2 tbsp dried thyme
1 tbsp flaky sea salt
2 tsp soft light brown sugar
1 tsp garlic powder
1 tsp ground cinnamon
2 tsp ground allspice
1 tsp ground ginger
2 tsp cayenne pepper
1 tsp ground black pepper
1 tsp grated nutmeg

For the pineapple slaw:
½ small white cabbage
2 carrots, peeled and grated
12 spring onions/scallions, shredded
300g/10½oz peeled, cored and finely diced ripe pineapple (prepared weight)
6 tbsp plain Greek yogurt
6 tbsp mayonnaise
sea salt and freshly ground black pepper

You will need to start your pork the day before. Combine all the spices for the jerk rub in a small bowl. Dry the skin of the pork belly with paper towels to remove as much moisture as you possibly can. Rub the jerk seasoning all over the pork belly, then wrap the meat in an open foil parcel so that the meat is covered but the skin is open to the air to dry it. Place the joint in a baking dish or similar and pop in the refrigerator to marinate overnight.

The next day, preheat the oven to 140°C/120°C fan/ 275°F/Gas 1. Keeping your pork parcel wrapped as it is, drizzle a little oil (about 1 teaspoon) over the skin of the pork and rub it evenly over the skin. Sprinkle over the salt and rub that in evenly too.

Place the pork in the oven and cook for 2½ hours. Halfway through this stage, remove the dish from the oven and tighten the foil around the sides of the pork to keep in the moisture as the piece will have shrunk and left a gap at the edge.

After the 2½ hours is up, tighten the foil again if necessary and crank up the heat to 240°C/ 220°C fan/475°F/Gas 9 to get the skin really crispy and achieve great crackling. Leave to rest in the foil parcel for 10 minutes before slicing.

To make the slaw, shred the cabbage, either on a mandoline or with a sharp knife. Put it in a large bowl and add all the remaining ingredients. Taste and season well with salt and pepper.

STICKY SCRUMPY RIBS

Sticky barbecue ribs is always a family favourite. For a summer vibe, I like to finish these over charcoal and add some scrumpy cider and star anise to the glaze for an appley flavour with liquorice undertones. It's hard to stop going back for more. Serve with a big salad and a few glasses of nice cold cider.

1 large rack meaty pork ribs (about 1.8kg/4lb in total)
6 star anise
300ml/10½fl oz/1¼ cups scrumpy cider
120ml/4fl oz/½ cup maple syrup
150g/5oz smooth jarred apple sauce (or blend it in a mini chopper/push it through a sieve/fine-mesh strainer)
sea salt and freshly ground black pepper

Preheat the oven to 160°C/140°C fan/320°F/Gas 3.

Season the ribs all over with salt and pepper and put them in a large shallow dish (such as a ceramic baking dish). Add the star anise and pour in the scrumpy cider. Cover the baking dish with foil, then place this dish in a larger roasting pan – this will help prevent you from sloshing hot cider over your hands when you remove the ribs from the oven. Place the pan in the middle of the oven and cook for 2 hours. Check them halfway through and add a little more cider if it looks like the ribs are getting dry.

Once the ribs are cooked, remove them from the cider and leave them to cool down a little. Tip about 100ml/3½fl oz/scant ½ cup of the cider into a wide saucepan (include the star anise) and set over a medium–high heat. Cook vigorously until the liquid reduces down to about half its volume, then fish out the star anise. Add the maple syrup and apple sauce to the pan and keep cooking until you have a sticky glaze. Taste and season well with salt and pepper.

Line a baking sheet with foil. If you are browning the ribs under the grill/broiler, preheat it to high. Otherwise, and ideally, get a barbecue ready. Place the ribs on the foil and pour the glaze over both sides, using a brush to spread it out evenly. Either place the baking sheet under the grill or put the ribs straight onto the barbecue rack and cook, turning over halfway through, on both sides until the glaze is sticky and charred in places. Slice the rack into individual ribs and serve.

MATZO KEEMA
KUGEL

Kugel is a traditional Polish dish that features heavily in the cuisines of its neighbouring cultures, so you see many variations as it spreads through the diaspora. Usually, it is a combination of potatoes and/or noodles with onions and often a minced/ground meat layer. In Jewish culture it is a traditional Ashkenazi dish. I've taken it to a new dimension with some intriguing swaps. Like tortilla chips or *totopos* in Mexican nachos, the matzo crackers in this kugel (taking the place of the more usual *lokshen* – egg noodles) bring another interesting texture to the mix. And a gently spiced Indian keema swapped in for the more classic meat completes this entirely international mash-up for an unexpected meal, ideal for a weeknight store-cupboard supper.

3 tbsp vegetable oil

2 onions, finely diced

5cm/2in piece of fresh root ginger, peeled and grated

4 garlic cloves, crushed

½ tsp ground turmeric

¼ tsp chilli powder

2 heaped tsp ground cumin

2½ tsp garam masala

500g/1lb 2oz minced/ground lamb

1 x 400g/14oz can chopped tomatoes

a handful of fresh or frozen peas

1 tsp salt

½ tsp sugar (any type)

1 large green chilli, deseeded and finely diced

a large handful of fresh coriander/cilantro, roughly chopped, plus extra to serve

For the crust:

4 eggs, lightly beaten

1 tsp salt

½ tsp grated nutmeg

150g/5oz matzo crackers

Pour the oil into a large frying pan over a medium heat. Add the onions and fry for 5 minutes until starting to soften, then add the ginger, garlic and dried spices and cook for a further 3 minutes until everything is smelling aromatic.

Add the lamb to the pan and continue to cook until it is browned; break up any large lumps with a spatula as it cooks. Add the tomatoes, peas, salt, sugar and 200ml/7fl oz/scant 1 cup water and continue to simmer gently for 15 minutes.

Meanwhile, start to make the crust. Mix the eggs, salt and nutmeg with 100ml/3½fl oz/scant ½ cup water in a bowl. Roughly break up the crackers and mix them into the bowl, leaving them to soak while the lamb simmers.

Stir the fresh chilli and coriander into the keema and tip the mixture into a baking dish. Tip the egg and matzo mix over the top. Bake the kugel for 25–30 minutes until the top is golden brown, then serve sprinkled with a little extra coriander.

OXTAIL AND COFFEE PIE

For a rich, roasted flavour to the gravy in your pie, it's a great idea to use some coffee in your stock. I use espresso from a old-fashioned coffee machine, but you could use a couple of pods of strong coffee too. This is family comfort food at its best.

3 tbsp olive oil

1kg/2lb 4oz oxtail pieces

300g/10½oz beef shin, cut into bite-sized chunks

1 large onion, finely sliced

a large sprig of fresh rosemary

a few sprigs of fresh thyme

2 large garlic cloves, finely chopped

2 large carrots, peeled and thickly sliced

½ celeriac, peeled and diced (about 400g/14oz prepared weight)

500ml/17fl oz/2 cups beef stock

100ml/3½fl oz/scant ½ cup strong espresso coffee

1 tbsp cornflour/cornstarch

1 tbsp honey

1 egg, beaten, for glazing

sea salt and freshly ground black pepper

For the rough puff pastry:

130g/4oz/1 cup plain/all-purpose flour, plus extra for dusting

a pinch of salt

100g/3½oz cold butter, cut into 1cm/½in cubes

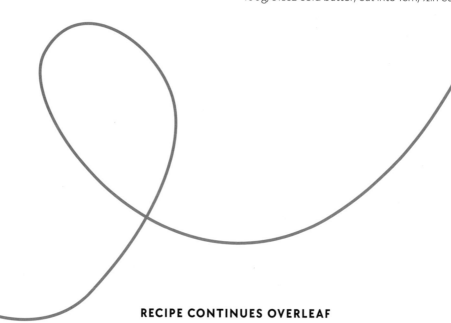

RECIPE CONTINUES OVERLEAF

Preheat the oven to 160°C/140°C fan/325°F/Gas 3 and find yourself a large casserole dish with a lid.

Heat 1 tablespoon of the olive oil over a high heat and add half the oxtail to the pan. Cook for a few minutes, turning the pieces frequently with tongs, until browned all over, then remove to a plate. Repeat to brown the second half of the oxtail, then remove from the pan again.

Add the beef shin to the pan, along with another 1 tablespoon of oil if you feel it needs it. Brown in the same way, then transfer to the plate with the oxtail.

Reduce the heat to low and add the onion, rosemary and thyme to the pan. Sauté gently for 6 minutes or so, until the onion is really soft and tender. Add the garlic, carrots and celeriac, sauté for a minute or so, then add the stock and coffee, season well with salt and pepper, and pop the lid on the pan. Transfer the casserole to the oven and cook for 2½ hours until the meat is meltingly tender. Remove from the oven and leave to cool to room temperature.

Meanwhile, make the pastry. Sift the flour and salt into a large bowl and add the cubed butter. Stir with a round-bladed knife to combine, then add 4 tablespoons of the water. Continue stirring to bring it all together, adding a little more water if you need to. Knead gently to bring it together, then roll it out on a flour-dusted work surface into a long rectangle with a short end toward you. Fold the bottom third up and the top third of the rectangle down, then turn it 90 degrees clockwise so you have a book shape with the pages on the right-hand side. Roll it out again to the same rectangle shape

and repeat the process, folding up, then down and turning. Do the process two more times, so you have done four rolls and folds in total – by this point, the butter should be incorporated and the pastry will be looking a lot neater. Wrap it in cling film/plastic wrap and pop it in the refrigerator until required.

Once the casserole is cool, remove the oxtail from the pan and pull the meat from the bones. Stir the meat back into the pie filling (ensuring you don't add any tough cartilage back into the pot) and discard the bones. Extract any tough herb stalks from the casserole, too. Slake the cornflour with a splash of cold water and stir it in along with the honey. Taste and adjust the seasoning, if necessary.

When you are ready to assemble and bake your pie, preheat the oven to 210°C/190°C fan/410°F/Gas 7. Tip the filling into a 1.25-litre/5-cup pie dish with a wide lip. Place a pie funnel in the middle of the dish.

Roll out the pastry on a flour-dusted work surface and use it to cover the top of the pie, trimming the excess around the edge with a sharp knife and crimping the edge to seal. Make a hole in the middle of the pie that lines up with the hole in the pie funnel. Use any offcuts of pastry to decorate the top of the pie using a little of the beaten egg to stick them onto the pie. Glaze the whole top of the pie with beaten egg and place it in the oven. Bake for about 15 minutes, then turn the temperature down to 200°C/180°C/400°F/Gas 6 and bake for a further 25–30 minutes until the pastry is risen and golden, and the filling is piping hot throughout.

BLACK PUDDING MOLE MEATBALLS

Bump up the flavour of your meatballs with black pudding and chocolate, and serve them Mexican style with a thick, rich, mole sauce. The truly bold can try it with 100% cocoa chocolate, which is very authentic but slightly more bitter-tasting. For a smoother result, 75% chocolate is just as good. You can make the meatballs and cook them and the sauce in the same pan so all the tasty meat juices get added to the sauce. This is a simplified mole sauce as authentic versions can have up to 50 ingredients. Here served with polenta/cornmeal, but a zippy green salad wouldn't go amiss either.

2 tbsp olive oil, plus extra if needed

1 small onion, finely diced

1 tsp dried Mexican oregano (or use regular oregano if you can't find it)

1 garlic clove, crushed

1 tbsp smoky chilli paste, such as ancho

400g/14oz minced/ground beef (not too lean)

100g/3½oz black pudding

30g/1oz very dark/bittersweet chocolate (75% cocoa solids minimum – 100% cocoa for the bolder palate, if you can find it), finely grated

about 4 tbsp fresh breadcrumbs, plus extra if needed

1 small egg, lightly beaten

sea salt and freshly ground black pepper

For the simplified mole sauce:

10 dried guajillo chillies

1 onion, finely diced

2 garlic cloves, finely chopped

2 tsp Mexican oregano

1 tbsp ancho chilli paste

1 tsp ground cumin

½ tsp ground cinnamon

1 x 400g/14oz can chopped tomatoes

200ml/7fl oz/scant 1 cup beef stock

1 tbsp honey

30g/1oz dark/bittersweet chocolate, finely grated

2 tbsp smooth peanut butter

sea salt and freshly ground black pepper

To serve:

cooked soft polenta/cornmeal

chopped fresh coriander/cilantro

lime wedges

RECIPE CONTINUES OVERLEAF

Start by preparing the chillies for the sauce. Heat a dry large sauté pan over a high heat. Once hot, toast the dried chillies for a few seconds on each side (don't let them burn) until smelling smoky. Pop them in a heatproof bowl and cover with boiling water from the kettle. Leave for 30 minutes to soften.

Meanwhile, make the meatballs, heat 1 tablespoon of the oil in the same sauté pan over a low–medium heat and add the onion. Cook for 7 minutes or so, until the onion is soft and translucent, then add the oregano, garlic and chilli paste, and cook for another couple of minutes. Turn off the heat and leave the mixture to cool a little.

Put the beef in a large bowl and crumble in the black pudding. Stir in the cooled onion mixture, chocolate and breadcrumbs. Add the egg and mix everything with your hands – really mushing it together until it starts to clump. If the mixture is too wet, add more breadcrumbs. Season well with salt and pepper, then divide the mixture into 16 even portions and roll them into balls.

In the same pan as you cooked the onion, heat the remaining 1 tablespoon of the oil. Add the meatballs to the pan and cook them over a medium heat, turning regularly with tongs, until they are browned all over and cooked through. Remove to a plate.

Add the onion for the sauce to the pan, adding a little extra oil if you need to. Cook for a few minutes until the onion is softening, then add the garlic, Mexican oregano, ancho chilli paste, cumin and cinnamon. Cook for a couple more minutes until everything is smelling aromatic.

Strain the soaked chillies and roughly chop them, discarding any stalks as you go. Put them in a blender or food processor and add the chopped tomatoes. Add the onion mixture from the pan and blend until everything is smooth, then return the mixture to the pan. Stir in the beef stock, honey, chocolate and peanut butter and season with salt and pepper.

Return the meatballs to the pan, along with any juices that have gathered on the plate, stir in, then leave everything to bubble away for 15–20 minutes, or until the sauce has thickened and the meatballs are cooked through. Adjust the seasoning, if you need to, and serve over polenta with chopped coriander and a squeeze of lime.

KASHMIRI CRUSTED COTE DE BOEUF

Perk up Sunday lunch with some full-on flavour, with a spiced rub for the meat plus anchovies and smoke in the butter. I sometimes serve this alongside a nice grain salad and spiced roasted veg, but it's also great with a leafy salad. No need to smoke your own butter – you can buy this in the frozen section of some supermarkets now.

1kg/2lb 4oz cote de boeuf, at room temperature
a little olive oil, for drizzling

For the Kashmiri spice rub:
1 tsp cumin seeds
2 tsp coriander seeds
1 tsp fennel seeds
seeds from 4 cardamom pods
1 tsp whole black peppercorns
4 whole dried Kashmiri chillies
a good pinch of flaky sea salt
½ tsp ground cinnamon
a good pinch of ground cloves
a good pinch of ground nutmeg

For the smoked anchovy butter:
5 anchovy fillets, finely chopped
50g/2oz smoked butter, softened

First make the Kashmiri spice rub. Toast the cumin, coriander, fennel and cardamom seeds, peppercorns and whole chillies in a dry frying pan for a few minutes until smelling toasty and the cumin seeds are a deep brown. Tip them into a pestle and mortar or spice grinder with a good pinch of the salt and coarsely grind. You may need to tip out the seeds and give the chillies a good go on their own to grind them down to flakes. Add the ground spices to the mixture and stir everything together.

Drizzle the cote de boeuf with a little oil and rub it all over, then sprinkle the spice mix all over the joint, remembering the thick edges too, making sure it is fully covered. Place it in a dish, cover and leave to marinate in the refrigerator for at least 4 hours, but leave time to remove it from the refrigerator and let it get back up to room temperature before cooking.

Meanwhile, make the smoked anchovy butter by simply mixing the anchovies into the softened butter in a small bowl. Scoop it onto a sheet of greaseproof/wax paper in a line and roll up, shaping it into a neat sausage as you go. Twist the ends to seal and refrigerate until it has firmed up.

To cook the beef, preheat the oven to 220°C/ 200°C fan/425°F/Gas 7 and place an ovenproof ridged griddle/grill pan over a high heat. Once very hot, add the cote de boeuf and sear for about 3 minutes on each side – plus another 1 minute or so on the edge to crisp up the fat – until it is caramelising and starting to char. Transfer the griddle to the oven and cook for another 16 minutes.

Remove the beef from the heavy pan straight away (or it will keep cooking) and let it rest on a board. Slice the butter into discs and allow them to melt over the hot beef to serve.

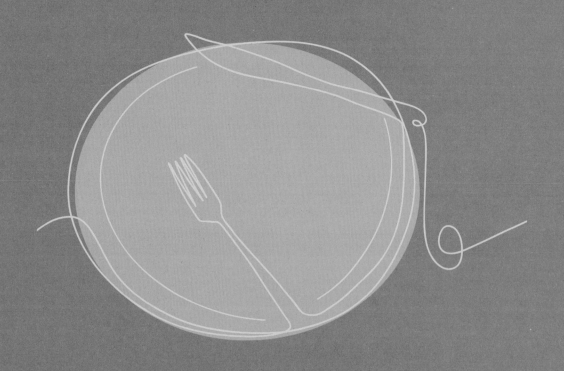

SWEET PLATES

CHERRY AND BLACK PEPPER MALT LOAF

An unusual take on the traditional malt loaf, this dried cherry version has an added daring addition of black pepper for heat and complexity. Slice and serve spread with some good salted butter for a teatime treat.

You can eat it straight away if wished, but I find it's best if kept wrapped in baking parchment for a couple of days before enjoying, which allows the flavours and stickiness to intensify.

butter, for greasing and serving
150g/5oz dried cherries
100ml/3½fl oz/scant ½ cup hot, strong black tea
7 tbsp malt extract
2 tbsp black treacle
180g/6½oz/1¼ cups wholemeal self-raising flour
½ tsp ground mixed spice
1 tsp freshly ground black pepper
1 egg

Preheat the oven to 140°C/120°C fan/275°F/Gas 1. Grease a 900g/2lb loaf tin with butter and line with baking parchment.

First, put the dried cherries in a small bowl with the hot tea, malt extract and treacle, stir well and set aside for at least 10 minutes.

Sift the flour into a mixing bowl and add the mixed spice and black pepper.

Crack the egg into the cooled malt mixture and whisk together, then pour the wet ingredients into the dry ones and fold everything together.

Pour the batter into the prepared loaf tin and spread level. Bake the loaf for about 1 hour 20 minutes, or until a skewer inserted into the middle of the loaf comes out clean.

Leave the loaf to cool in the tin for a few minutes before turning it out onto a wire/cooling rack to cool completely. While you can eat it straight away, it will really benefit from being wrapped in baking parchment at this point and left for a couple of days before enjoying.

Serve the loaf sliced, preferably slathered in butter.

ORANGE AND CARDAMOM LIVERPOOL TART

The first mention of the recipe for a Liverpool Tart dates back to a hand-written family cookbook from 1897. Famous for its use of whole boiled and minced lemons and dark muscovado/brown sugar, the original tarts are often seen in local bakeries, topped with a stencil of the famous Liver Bird, the symbol of my hometown city. The original recipe, which cooks the fruit whole, pith and all, is a bold step already, but I've swapped in tangy oranges and a heady hit of floral cardamom to take it to new heights. It's rich and delicious; perfect served cold for afternoon tea or as a warm pudding with plenty of whipped cream on the side.

For the filling:
2 blood oranges or regular oranges
125g/4oz unsalted butter, softened
200g/7oz/scant 1 cup caster/superfine sugar
2 medium eggs, at room temperature
seeds of 4 cardamom pods, finely crushed

For the sweet shortcrust pastry:
150g/5oz/1¼ cups plain/all-purpose flour
100g/3½oz salted butter, chilled and cubed
45g/1¾oz/scant ¼ cup caster/superfine sugar
1 small egg yolk

To serve (optional):
whipped cream

First, start the filling as the oranges will take a while to cook. Put the oranges in a small saucepan and pour over enough boiling water from the kettle so that they are just covered. Put them over a low–medium heat and leave them to simmer for 1 hour until the skins are soft, topping up with more hot water if it starts to get low.

Meanwhile, make the pastry. Put the flour and the cubes of butter in a food processor and pulse until the mixture has a crumb-like texture. Add the sugar and quickly pulse in to combine, then add the egg yolk and 1 tablespoon water. Blitz again until the dough comes together into a ball – you may have to add a drizzle more water. Once it's clumping together, tip it onto a work surface and finish bringing it together with your hands, then flatten into a round patty, wrap in cling film/plastic wrap and leave to chill for 30 minutes.

Roll out the chilled pastry and use it to line a 20cm/8in tart tin that's at least 3cm/1in deep. Prick the base with a fork and return it to the refrigerator to chill for another 20 minutes. Preheat the oven to 190°C/170°C fan/350°F/Gas 5.

Once the oranges are cooked, drain them and set aside until they are cool enough to handle.

Line the chilled tart case with a sheet of baking parchment and baking beans/pie weights and blind bake for 12 minutes, making sure the paper covers the edges of the tin too so the sides of the pastry don't overcook. Remove the parchment and the beans/weights and return to the oven for another 10 minutes, or until the base is lightly golden. Remove the tin from the oven and reduce the temperature to 170°C/150°C fan/325°F/Gas 3.

Roughly chop the cooked oranges, removing any pips as you go, and place the pieces in a food processor with the butter, sugar, eggs and cardamom. Blitz until smooth.

Pour the filling into the pastry case and pop it in the oven to bake for 20–25 minutes, until the filling is set but there's still a little wobble in the middle. Leave to cool and set before serving.

MARMITE CARAMEL BLONDIES

The tang the Marmite brings to the caramel swirl running through these blondies is unusual, but I know you will be pleasantly surprised by the flavour. Just like a good salted caramel, the slight saltiness of the Marmite combined with the natural bitterness of the walnuts enhances and offsets the sweetness of the blondie. If you're wary of making your own caramel, you could of course use shop-bought caramel or dulce de leche and stir the Marmite through. The caramel sinks into the batter slightly on cooking and you end up with a cinder toffee effect on top. Sticky, delicious, moreish.

175g/6oz/scant 1½ cups plain/all-purpose flour
½ tsp baking powder
180g/6½oz salted butter, melted and cooled
280g/10oz/generous 1¼ cups light brown sugar
2 eggs
2 tsp vanilla extract
100g/3½oz/generous ¾ cup chopped walnuts

For the Marmite caramel:
125g/4oz/generous ½ cup caster/superfine sugar
30g/1oz salted butter
100ml/3½fl oz/scant ½ cup double/heavy cream
2 tbsp Marmite

First make the caramel, so it's ready for when you need it. Put 4 tablespoons of water in a saucepan and tip in the sugar. Place the pan over a medium heat and stir gently until the sugar has dissolved, then leave it to cook for 5 minutes or so, without stirring, until it is a lovely golden colour. Throw in the butter and let it melt in, then remove the pan from the heat and stir in the cream. It may spit at first, but keep stirring until you have a smooth sauce. Once fully combined, stir in the Marmite, transfer the mixture to a pouring jug and set aside to cool.

For the blondies, preheat the oven to 180°C/160°C fan/350°F/Gas 4. Line a 20 x 30cm/8 x 12in brownie tin with baking parchment.

Sift the flour and baking powder into a bowl.

In another bowl, stir together the melted butter and sugar. Once combined, stir in the eggs and vanilla extract. Add the flour mixture and fold in, then fold in the chopped walnuts. Pour the mixture into the prepared brownie tin and spread level.

If the caramel has set too much and is no longer pourable, heat it gently for a few seconds to loosen it up. Drizzle the caramel all over the top of the blondie, then stir it gently through with the handle of a spoon or a skewer to create a marbled effect in the batter.

Bake the blondie for about 30 minutes, or until the mixture is just set.

Leave to cool for a few minutes in the tin before transferring to a wire/cooling rack to cool completely. Once cool, slice into 12 squares. Store in an airtight tin for up to three days.

SINGAPORE SLING PINEAPPLE UPSIDE-DOWN CAKE

Combining those tropical flavours you get in a good Singapore Sling (pineapple, bitters, cherry liqueur...), this lovely cake has a gorgeously strong punch of lime cutting through the sweetness. A fun dessert that doesn't take itself too seriously, there is something very retro about it that I love.

Tip: It's essential you *don't* take the cake out the tin while still warm, or it will fall apart. It needs to stay in the tin until completely cold, to soak up the drizzle and firm up.

For the tin:

50g/2oz butter, plus extra for greasing

7 canned pineapple rings in syrup

50g/2oz/¼ cup light muscovado/brown sugar

13 Maraschino cherries (or use cocktail cherries)

For the cake:

150g/5oz unsalted butter, softened

150g/5oz/⅔ cup caster/superfine sugar

3 eggs, beaten

150g/5oz/1¼ cups self-raising flour

½ tsp baking powder

a pinch of salt

1 tsp vanilla extract

For the drizzle:

2 limes

3 tbsp gin

½ tsp Angostura bitters

1 tbsp caster/superfine sugar

Preheat the oven to 190°C/170°C fan/375°F/Gas 5 and butter and line a 20cm/8in cake tin with baking parchment.

Drain the pineapple slices, reserving the syrup. Leave one ring whole, but slice the other six rings in half to get 12 semi-circles, then set aside on paper towels.

Melt the butter for the tin in a saucepan, then stir in the muscovado sugar. Pour the mixture into the prepared tin and spread level. Arrange the pineapple slices in the tin, placing the whole ring in the middle and the crescents around the outside. Add a cherry to each hole.

To make the sponge, cream together the butter and caster sugar in a stand mixer fitted with a paddle, until light and fluffy. Add the beaten eggs a little at a time, mixing well between each addition.

Sift the flour and baking powder into the bowl and add the salt, vanilla extract and 2 tablespoons of the reserved pineapple syrup. Fold everything together until you have a smooth batter. Pour the batter into the tin, being very careful not to dislodge the pineapple and cherries, and gently spread level. Bake for 30–35 minutes, or until golden on top, risen and a skewer inserted into the middle of the cake comes out clean.

While the cake is baking, make the drizzle. Grate the lime zest and set it aside, then juice the lime. Put the lime juice in a small saucepan with the gin, Angostura bitters, caster sugar and 2 tablespoons of the pineapple syrup from the can. Heat gently for a couple of minutes until the sugar is dissolved.

When the cake comes out of the oven, immediately poke holes all over the top with a skewer and pour the drizzle over. Leave to cool completely, then invert the cake onto a plate. Sprinkle over the lime zest to finish.

THYME APPLE TART CAKE
WITH RUM BUTTERSCOTCH SAUCE

The pastry layer that forms the base of this cake sets it texturally apart from your standard cake, giving it tart vibes. Fresh thyme lends its gentle herbal notes to lift the apple, but the real hero here is the rum butterscotch sauce, which brings a warming heat and is so delicious it's hard to stop yourself pouring a bit more, and a bit more, and a bit more... Go on, treat yourself.

1 sheet ready-rolled puff pastry
175g/6oz unsalted butter, plus extra for greasing
175g/6oz/¾ cup caster/superfine sugar
3 eggs
175g/6oz/scant 1½ cups plain/all-purpose flour
2 tsp baking powder
1 tsp ground mixed spice
4 Granny Smith apples
4 tsp finely chopped fresh thyme leaves
juice of ½ lemon

For the rum butterscotch sauce:
50g/2oz unsalted butter
50g/2oz/¼ cup caster/superfine sugar
75g/2½oz/⅓ cup soft light brown sugar
150g/5oz/scant ½ cup golden syrup
120ml/4fl oz/½ cup double/heavy cream
3 tbsp dark rum

Preheat the oven to 220°C/200°C fan/425°F/Gas 7. Unroll the puff pastry and place it on a heavy baking sheet, still on its paper. Bake for about 12–15 minutes, or until risen and light golden, then leave to cool.

Turn the oven down to 180°C/160°C fan/350°F/Gas 4 and grease a deep 25 x 20cm/10 x 8in brownie tin with butter. Once the pastry is cool, trim it to a rectangle the size of the prepared tin, and place it in the base of the tin.

To make the sponge, cream together the butter and sugar until light and fluffy, then beat in the eggs. Sift the flour, baking powder and mixed spice into the mixture and fold in. Quickly peel and dice one of the apples and fold that in too, along with the thyme leaves. Spoon the batter over the pastry in the tin and spread it level.

Peel and core the remaining apples and slice each one in half. Lay the apple slices over the top of the batter in neat rows, then brush the slices with the lemon juice to prevent them turning brown.

Bake the cake for about 1 hour, or until firm to the touch. Check that a skewer inserted into the cake comes out clean.

While the cake is cooking, make the sauce. Put the butter, sugars and syrup in a saucepan and stir over a low–medium heat until melted. Cook for 5 minutes, then remove from the heat and pour in the cream. Once combined, add the rum and return the pan to the heat. Continue to cook gently for a few minutes, stirring, until thickened slightly.

Once baked, slice the cake and serve in squares with the rum butterscotch sauce to drizzle over.

TREACLE AND FENNEL TART

This stickily sweet treacle tart has a gorgeously savoury edge to it with the addition of fragrant anise-flavoured fennel seeds. Ideal for your next dinner party dessert with a pour of rich cream on the side.

1 x 375g/13oz sheet ready-rolled shortcrust pastry
1 tbsp fennel seeds
350g/12oz/1 cup golden syrup
finely grated zest of 1 lemon plus 2 tbsp juice
1 egg, lightly beaten
100g/3½oz/1¼ cups fresh breadcrumbs

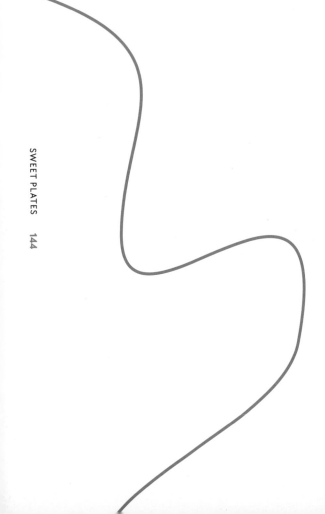

Use the pastry sheet to line a shallow 20cm/8in tart tin. Prick the base all over with a fork and chill for 30 minutes.

Meanwhile, preheat the oven to 220°C/200°C fan/ 425°F/Gas 7 and place a heavy baking sheet on the middle shelf to heat up with the oven.

Once chilled, line the pastry case with baking parchment and baking beans/pie weights and set it on the hot baking sheet. Bake for about 12 minutes, until starting to brown around the edges, then remove the beans/weights and return the case to the oven for a further 8–10 minutes until light golden. Leave to cool a little while you make the filling.

Reduce the oven temperature to 200°C/180°C fan/ 400°F/Gas 6.

Coarsely grind the fennel seeds in a pestle and mortar. You don't want a fine powder, nor whole seeds – something in between will give you an ambient flavour and the occasional pop of fennel, too. Tip them into a heavy saucepan, set it over a medium heat and toast the spices for a minute or so until smelling great.

Add the golden syrup to the pan and stir in the lemon zest and juice, wait a few seconds, then turn off the heat. The residual warmth of the pan should help loosen the syrup slightly. Stir in the egg, then very gently fold in the breadcrumbs. Leave for 5 minutes for the crumbs to absorb the syrup.

Tip the filling into the pastry case and spread level. Bake for 15–20 minutes, or until the filling is just set.

It will be volcanically hot, so leave to cool down a little before serving.

SPICED RUM AND RAISIN ECCLES CAKES

Easy, effective and delicious, this take on the traditional fruity Northern pastry is a rich treat with a boozy bonus edge from the spiced rum. Pair with a dry, crumbly Lancashire cheese for a taste of heaven.

500g/1lb 2oz ready-made puff pastry
plain/all-purpose flour, for dusting
1 egg, lightly beaten, for glazing
granulated sugar, to sprinkle

For the filling:
50g/2oz unsalted butter
250g/9oz/2 cups cup raisins
finely grated zest of 2 limes (or 1 orange)
80g/3oz/generous ⅓ cup soft light brown sugar
1 tsp ground cinnamon
1 tsp ground ginger
1 tsp ground nutmeg
½ tsp allspice
a good pinch of ground cloves
1 tsp vanilla extract
1 tbsp black treacle or molasses
4 tbsp golden rum

Melt the butter for the filling in a large saucepan over a low heat. Turn off the heat, add all the other filling ingredients and stir together well. Set aside for 1 hour, or ideally overnight, until completely cool and the liquid has been absorbed.

Preheat the oven to 200°C/180°C fan/400°F/Gas 6 and line a baking sheet with baking parchment.

Roll out the pastry on a lightly floured work surface to about 3mm/⅛in thick. Using a 9cm/3½in round pastry cutter, stamp out as many circles as possible – you should get 12–14 circles.

Divide the filling evenly between the discs, placing a large spoonful in the middle of each. Using a pastry brush, brush around the edge of each pastry disc with the beaten egg. Gather up the edges of each disc and bring them together to create a parcel. Press the pastry together well at the top to seal, then turn each parcel over so that the gathered pastry is hidden underneath and you have a nice smooth top. Gently roll each parcel with a rolling pin to flatten slightly, then transfer to the baking sheet. Using a very sharp knife, make three small slits in the top of each to allow the steam to escape and create the classic Eccles cake look. Brush each one with the beaten egg, then sprinkle generously with sugar.

Bake for about 25 minutes, or until the pastry is golden brown and crisp, and the filling is piping hot throughout. Leave to cool a little (the filling will be like molten lava) before serving warm.

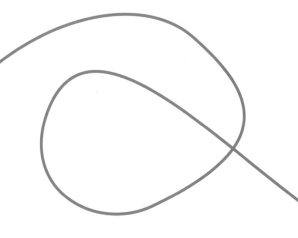

LEVANTINE TOFFEE APPLES

Citrussy sumac and tangy pomegranate molasses help to give the caramel a rich red colour and a Middle-Eastern flavour to these pretty toffee apples. As the molasses is slightly acidic, it helps stand in for the vinegar that is more ordinarily used. The sprinkles in the coating here could be swapped for other nuts, such as toasted flaked almonds or even sesame seeds – let your imagination run wild.

8 small–medium apples, such as Cox's
400g/14oz/1¾ cups caster/superfine sugar
4 tbsp pomegranate molasses
1 tbsp liquid glucose
1½ tsp sumac

For sprinkling and coating:
chopped pistachios (go for really green ones)
dried barberries (available from your local
   international grocers)

Before you start, get all your sprinkles ready – toasting, chopping, etc. – and set aside in small bowls. Line a baking sheet with non-stick baking parchment.

Put the apples in a heatproof bowl and pour boiling water over them. Let them sit for a minute or so, then drain them and dry well with paper towels. This will remove any wax on the skin and help the toffee to stick. Insert a lolly stick or skewer into each one.

Put the sugar, molasses and liquid glucose in a saucepan and add 100ml/3½fl oz/scant ½ cup water. Place the pan over a medium heat. Stir the mixture until the sugar dissolves, then leave the caramel to cook, without stirring (although you can swirl the pan if you need to) until the caramel reaches 150°C/300°F – or hard crack stage – on a sugar thermometer. At this stage, carefully stir in the sumac.

At this point, and working quickly, carefully tilt the pan so a deeper well of caramel collects on one side. Holding it by its lolly stick, swirl an apple in the caramel to coat it fully. Sprinkle the apple with your choice of sprinkles, then place it on the prepared baking sheet to set. Repeat to coat and decorate all your apples. If the caramel starts to set too hard, simply return it to the heat until it loosens again.

Leave the apples to set fully before enjoying.

PLUM AND TAMARIND STRUDEL

Tamarind and dried plums form the basis of a cooling summer sherbet recipe popular in India, Pakistan and the Middle East, so I wanted to see whether they would also work in dessert form. They do – the tamarind bringing an element of sharpness to the sweet plums, creating a very tasty combination. I think people are quite reluctant to make their own strudel pastry these days, so I've given you a recipe using ready-made filo/phyllo for ease.

90g/3¼oz unsalted butter
50g/2oz/⅔ cup fresh breadcrumbs
400g/14oz ripe plums, pitted and chopped
    into large dice
1 tbsp tamarind paste
a pinch of ground cloves
125g/4oz/generous ½ cup caster/superfine sugar,
    plus extra to sprinkle
6 sheets of ready-made filo/phyllo pastry
icing/confectioners' sugar, for dusting
cream or vanilla ice cream, to serve

Preheat the oven to 190°C/170°C fan/375°F/ Gas 5 and line a heavy baking sheet with baking parchment.

Melt 30g/1oz of the butter in a frying pan. Add the breadcrumbs and stir so they are all well coated in the butter. Cook over a medium heat, stirring frequently, until they are golden brown. Remove from the heat.

Put the plums in a bowl and add the tamarind paste, cloves, caster sugar and breadcrumbs. Stir until the plums are well coated with everything.

Melt the remaining butter, either in a pan or in the microwave. Lay a sheet of filo pastry on another sheet of baking parchment and brush it with the melted butter, then sprinkle it lightly with caster sugar. Lay another sheet on top and repeat the process. Continue to lay, brush and sprinkle until you have used all your pastry sheets.

Pile the plum filling along one long edge of the filo stack, leaving the ends clear by about 4cm/1½in. Fold the pastry at the ends in, then roll up the strudel, keeping the ends tucked in as you go. Carefully transfer the strudel, seam-side down, onto the prepared baking sheet, using the parchment to help you, and brush it all over with more melted butter.

Bake the strudel for 45–50 minutes, until golden brown all over and the filling is piping hot. Dust with icing sugar and serve in slices with cream or ice cream on the side.

SOUK SCONES

These Moroccan-style scones, heady with saffron and orange blossom, make a fragrant alternative to a traditional cream tea. Delicious served with an orange-scented whipped cream (whip in a drop or two of orange flower water and some grated orange zest) and some apricot jam.

120ml/4fl oz/½ cup whole milk, plus extra
   as needed
a large pinch of saffron strands
450g/1lb/3⅔ cups self-raising flour,
   plus extra for dusting
2 tsp baking powder
70g/2½oz/scant ⅓ cup caster/superfine sugar
a pinch of salt
150g/5oz unsalted butter, chilled and diced
150g/5oz dried apricots, chopped
1½ tsp orange flower water
1 beaten egg, for glazing

Preheat the oven to 220°C/200°C fan/425°F/Gas 7 and line a large baking sheet with baking parchment.

Warm 4 tablespoons of the milk gently for a few seconds in the microwave, then add the saffron, stir together and set aside to infuse.

Meanwhile, sift the flour and baking powder into a mixing bowl and add the sugar, a pinch of salt and the butter. Using your fingertips, rub the butter into the dry ingredients until the mixture resembles breadcrumbs, then stir in the apricots.

Slowly add the remaining 60ml/2fl oz/¼ cup milk, the infused saffron milk and the orange flower water, then carefully bring the dough together, pressing with your hands and making a few folds, being careful not to knead. Add another tablespoon or two of milk if you need it, but don't worry if the mix is a little crumbly.

Turn the dough out onto a flour-dusted work surface and, with a flour-dusted rolling pin, roll it out to about 3cm/1in thick. Using a 6cm/2½in round cutter, cut out as many scones as possible – you should get about 12 scones – placing them on the prepared baking sheet as you go.

Brush the top of the scones with the beaten egg and bake for about 12–15 minutes, or until risen and golden brown. Enjoy warm or leave to cool on the baking sheet, but they are best eaten the same day, or frozen for future enjoyment.

PARMA VIOLET CHOCOLATE MOUSSE

There is a lovely light texture to this velvety mousse. With its intensely floral hit of Parma Violets, it provides an unexpected flavour to liven up the tastebuds. Ideal to serve to dinner guests when entertaining.

150g/5oz dark/bittersweet chocolate (at least 70% cocoa solids), roughly chopped
90ml/3fl oz/6 tbsp hot water
2 large eggs, separated
30g/1oz/2 tbsp caster/superfine sugar
a few drops of violet extract, to taste (I use about 6–7)
100ml/3½fl oz/scant ½ cup double/heavy cream or whipping cream
1 small roll of Parma Violet sweets

Put the chocolate in a heatproof bowl, pour in the hot water and set the bowl over a pan of gently simmering water, making sure the base of the bowl is not touching the water. Leave to melt for a few minutes, stirring occasionally. Once smooth, remove the bowl from the pan and leave the chocolate to cool a little.

Meanwhile, put the egg whites in a perfectly clean bowl and whisk until soft peaks form. Start adding the sugar, a little at a time, and continue to whisk until all the sugar is incorporated and the egg whites are glossy and stiff.

Stir the egg yolks into the chocolate mixture until well incorporated, then add the violet extract, making it as strong as you dare.

With a large metal spoon, beat a couple of tablespoons of the egg white into the chocolate mixture to loosen it. Then, add the remaining egg white and fold it in gently, being careful not to knock all the air out of the mousse. Divide the mousse between four ramekin dishes or glasses and leave in the refrigerator to set.

Before serving, whip the cream to soft peaks. Roughly crush the Parma Violets, leaving some larger pieces. Serve the mousse pots with a blob of cream on top and sprinkle with the sweets to decorate.

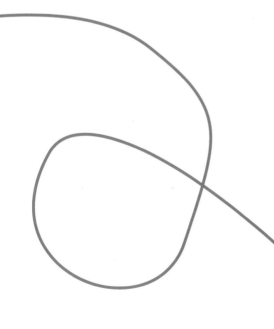

PEANUT AND GOOSEBERRY FOOL

An unusual combination, but I think the rich peanut butter is a great foil for the sharp gooseberry here, with little pops of peanut from the crunchy spread. Try to use a natural brand of peanut butter such as Whole Earth or Pip & Nut, rather than one loaded with sugar and other unnecessary additives.

400g/14oz gooseberries, topped and tailed
100g/3½oz/scant ½ cup caster/superfine sugar
200ml/7fl oz/scant 1 cup double/heavy cream
100ml/3½fl oz/scant ½ cup thick Greek yogurt
50g/2oz/scant ¼ cup crunchy peanut butter
a few roasted, salted peanuts, roughly chopped,
   to serve

Put the gooseberries in a saucepan with the sugar and cook, stirring frequently, over a low heat, until they have broken down and are mushy – about 10 minutes. Remove from the heat and leave to cool, then place in the refrigerator to chill.

Once your fruit mixture is cold, put the cream into a bowl and whip until at soft peak stage. Be very careful not to over-whip it as it will keep whipping as you fold in the other ingredients.

Fold the yogurt into the cream, then swirl in the gooseberry purée.

Put the peanut butter in a small bowl and microwave for a few seconds. You don't want it hot or it will melt the cream, but just loose enough to stir through.

Place a good dollop of the fool into four glass serving dishes. Spoon an equal amount of the peanut butter on top of each, then top each with another spoonful of the fool. Swirl very gently, then sprinkle with the peanuts and chill before serving.

MANGO CRUMBLE
WITH MINT CREAM

Apple crumble step aside, this summery mango crumble has it all going on. A rich, sunshine-yellow interior, with a hint of rum and lime, topped with a coconutty rubble and a soft mint cream. Sumptuously yummy.

1 x 850g/1lb 14oz can alphonso mango, diced into 1.5cm/⅝in cubes
1½ tbsp cornflour/cornstarch
40g/1½oz/3 tbsp caster/superfine sugar
grated zest of 1 lime
2 tbsp coconut rum

For the crumble:
120g/4oz/1 cup plain/all-purpose flour
80g/3oz butter, diced and chilled
75g/2½oz/scant ⅓ cup caster/superfine sugar
75g/2½oz/generous ¾ cup desiccated/dried shredded coconut
a pinch of salt

For the cream:
a few fresh mint leaves, to taste
150ml/5fl oz/scant ⅔ cup double/heavy cream
2 tbsp icing/confectioners' sugar

Preheat the oven to 190°C/170°C fan/375°F/Gas 5 and find yourself a 23cm/9in round baking dish (or dish of equivalent volume).

Tip the mango pieces into the baking dish, and sprinkle over the cornflour, sugar and lime zest. Pour in the rum and mix until everything is well combined. Set aside while you make the crumble.

Put the flour in a mixing bowl and add the diced cold butter. Using your fingertips, rub the butter into the flour until it looks like breadcrumbs, then stir in the sugar, desiccated coconut and salt.

Sprinkle the crumble over the fruit in the dish, creating clumps as you go by squeezing the crumble mix in your fingers, which will give you a nice chunky rubble. Bake for about 45 minutes, or until the crumble is golden.

Meanwhile, make the mint cream. Very finely chop the mint and add it to the cream along with the icing sugar. Whip the cream until soft peaks form.

Once the crumble is baked, serve warm with dollops of the whipped mint cream.

FLOATING PACIFIC ISLANDS

Playing on the theme of *îles flotantes*, these light, whipped meringues floating in a lagoon of coconut- and pandan-flavoured custard will whisk you away to the tropics. Hailing from South-east Asia, pandan extract has a grassy fragrance with hints of rose, almond and vanilla flavour, verging on coconut, and lends a beautiful green hue to the custard. I have given instructions for making your own extract, but you can also buy it from Asian grocers if you prefer.

50g/2oz pandan leaves (or 60ml/2fl oz/¼ cup store-bought pandan extract)
30g/1oz coconut flakes, to serve

For the meringues:
2 egg whites
¼ tsp cream of tartar
½ tsp vanilla extract
80g/3oz/⅓ cup caster/superfine sugar
600ml/20fl oz/2½ cups good-quality coconut milk

For the coconut custard:
2 eggs plus 3 egg yolks
80g/3oz/⅓ cup caster/superfine sugar
1 tsp cornflour/cornstarch

To make the pandan extract, wash the leaves well, then roughly chop them into small pieces. Pop them in a blender (or mini chopper) and add 2 tablespoons water. Blend until you have a smooth paste. You may need to add more water or keep stopping the blender and using a spatula to push the ingredients back to the bottom, but once it has all taken, you can leave it to blend until smooth.

Line a sieve/fine-mesh strainer with a piece of muslin/cheesecloth and pour the pandan paste into it. Let it drain for a while, then twist the muslin to squeeze out the last of the liquid through the sieve. Discard the pulp. You should have about 60ml/ 2fl oz/¼ cup concentrated pandan juice.

To make the meringues, whisk the egg whites and cream of tartar until soft peak stage. Add the vanilla extract and whisk in, then add the sugar, a spoonful at a time, while whisking continuously. Continue beating the meringue until it is firm and glossy.

Pour the coconut milk into a wide saucepan and warm to a gentle simmer – be careful not to boil it. Scoop large spoonfuls of the meringue and drop them into the hot milk (you may have to cook these in batches – depending on how large your spoon is you should get 4–6 large meringues from the mixture). Cook over a low heat, uncovered, for about 5 minutes until the meringues are firm. Cover with the lid if you think they aren't cooking through. Remove them from the milk using a slotted spoon and place them on a plate to cool.

For the coconut custard, rewarm the milk you used for poaching the meringues, if it has cooled. Meanwhile, beat together the eggs, egg yolks, sugar and cornflour in a heatproof bowl.

Adding in a slow trickle while whisking all the time, pour about a quarter of the warm milk into the bowl with the eggs. Whisk in, then pour this mixture back into the saucepan. Cook gently, stirring constantly, until the mixture thickens.

Take off the heat and leave to cool slightly, stirring every now and then. Once it's at room temperature, add the pandan extract and stir through, then pour the custard into a bowl and cover the surface with cling film/plastic wrap. Chill until ready to serve.

While the custard and meringues are cooling, lightly toast the coconut flakes in a dry frying pan. Remove from the pan and set aside until ready to serve.

To serve, spoon a pool of custard into shallow bowls and place a meringue into each bowl. Sprinkle with the toasted coconut flakes.

CANDIED BACON AND BOURBON ICE CREAM

This is totally delicious. You may be slightly suspicious of the idea of 'bacon ice cream' but don't knock it 'til you've tried it. Candied bacon – salty and sweet – is a taste revelation and matches with the pecans just perfectly. The addition of bourbon, besides the obvious flavour benefits, means the ice cream is soft enough to scoop without leaving it to stand for an age, which is usually a problem with homemade ice cream, so win win. A grown-up treat.

For the candied bacon and pecans:

200g/7oz smoked streaky bacon
2 handful of pecans
3 tbsp maple syrup
2 tbsp soft dark brown sugar

For the ice cream:

600ml/20fl oz/2½ cups double/heavy cream
397g/14oz can condensed milk
1 tsp vanilla bean paste
3 tbsp bourbon whiskey

To serve:

maple syrup

First, candy your bacon and pecans. Preheat the oven to 200°C/180°C fan/400°F/Gas 6. Line a lipped baking sheet with foil.

Toss the bacon and pecans with the maple syrup and sugar, then spread out on the prepared baking sheet and bake for 10 minutes, or until the bacon is golden and crispy. Leave to cool completely, then finely chop with a knife.

Using a stand mixer fitted with a whisk, whip the double cream until it thickens and is soft and peaky. Continuing to whip, add the condensed milk and vanilla bean paste, and whip until incorporated and thickened. Add the whiskey and whip again – the cream should be thick and pillowy. Stir though the chopped bacon and pecans, reserving a small handful to sprinkle on top.

Pour into a large loaf tin, Tupperware or ice cream tub. Sprinkle the reserved bacon and pecans on top and freeze for 4 hours, or overnight.

Scoop into bowls and drizzle with maple syrup to serve.

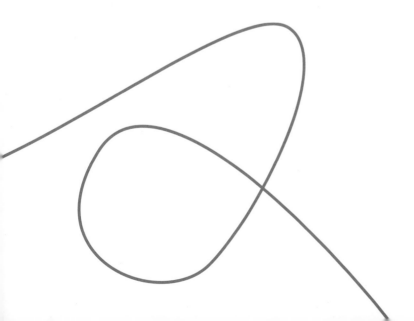

BANANA AND TAHINI BREAD AND BUTTER PUDDING

Not everyone is a fan of raisins, so I wondered what else I could add to a classic bread and butter pud. I instantly thought of banana – pillowy and sweet, and eternal friend to honey and cinnamon, they work beautifully in this comfort-food classic. The earthy sesame flavour of tahini grounds the sweetness for an added twist.

50g/2oz butter, plus extra for greasing
8 slices slightly stale white bread
about 100g/3½oz tahini, for spreading
2 large bananas, sliced on the diagonal
demerara/turbinado sugar, to sprinkle
1 tbsp sesame seeds

For the custard:
300ml/10½fl oz/1¼ cups whole milk
250ml/9fl oz/1 cup double/heavy cream
3 large eggs
3 tbsp caster/superfine sugar
2 tbsp runny honey
1 tbsp tahini
1 tsp vanilla extract
½ tsp ground cinnamon, plus extra for dusting

Grease a 20 x 25cm/8 x 10in baking dish with butter.

To make the custard, put the milk and cream in a saucepan and heat over a gentle heat until scalding point (almost but not yet boiling).

Meanwhile, in a heatproof jug, whisk together the eggs and sugar, then add the honey, tahini, vanilla extract and cinnamon and whisk again.

Very slowly pour the hot milk and cream into the jug, whisking all the time so that the eggs are tempered and they don't curdle. Keep whisking until all the liquid is added and the honey and tahini have dissolved, then set aside.

Slice the crusts off the bread and slice them diagonally into triangles. Spread each triangle with butter and layer half of them over the base of the baking dish. Drizzle half the tahini over the bread. Lay the banana slices on top of the bread, then repeat by placing the remaining bread on top of the bananas, and drizzling over the remaining tahini. Pour the custard over the bread, then set aside for 30 minutes for the custard to soak into the bread.

Meanwhile, preheat the oven to 180°C/160°C fan/350°F/Gas 4.

Once the 30 minutes are up, sprinkle the top of the pudding generously with demerara sugar, the sesame seeds and a pinch of cinnamon. Bake for about 40 minutes, until the top of the pudding is golden and it is risen slightly.

Serve immediately.

WOODLAND WITCH'S FROTH

This might be more familiar to some as Apple Snow – an old-fashioned, but deliciously light and refreshing dessert. I thought I'd go down the Hallowe'en route and spook it up into a Witch's Froth, flavoured with pine syrup for a hint of the deep dark forest, and we all know about fairytale witches affinity to apples...

If you don't have pine to garnish, a sprig of rosemary will do. And go easy with the pine syrup – you don't want it 'pine-fresh' – a subtle hint is all that's needed. You can buy pine syrup in posh drinks shops nowadays, sold as a mixer for cocktails.

450g/1lb baking apples, such as Bramley
   (about 2 large ones)
1 large egg white
60g/2¼oz/generous ¼ cup caster/superfine sugar
1 tbsp pine syrup, or to taste
a few sprigs of fresh pine (or rosemary) and
   dried apple rings, to decorate (optional)

Preheat the oven to 180°C/160°C fan/350°F/Gas 4. Place the apples in a roasting pan and transfer to the oven. Bake for about 40 minutes, or until completely tender and a knife inserted into an apple faces little resistance. Let the apples cool completely.

Remove all the flesh from the apples and put it in a bowl, discarding the cores and skin as you go. Using a potato ricer (or just a potato masher), mash the apple flesh to a pulp. Don't worry if there are a few small lumps in there – these all add to the texture.

Add the egg white and sugar to the bowl and use a stand mixer with a balloon whisk attachment or an electric hand whisk to whisk until the mixture is thick and fluffy – like apple meringue.

Add the pine syrup to the bowl (go easy, adding a drop or two at a time, to taste) and whisk for another few minutes until everything is incorporated and thickened up.

Spoon the froth into four glass serving dishes, dividing it equally, then finish with a sprig of pine and a dried apple ring to garnish, if wished. Place in the refrigerator and chill for an hour before serving. Eat the same day or the froth will begin to split.

PEPPERY PINK GRAPEFRUIT PAVLOVAS WITH SWEET ROCKET DRIZZLE

An elegant dinner party dessert if ever there was one, this is a true taste revelation. The peppery, mown-grass, herbal flavour of the rocket/arugula drizzle offsets the tooth-tingling sweetness of the meringue and all is smoothed out richly with the cream. It's my new favourite spring-into-summer showstopping pud.

You can of course use shop-bought meringue nests for the base if you wish, although they tend to be quite small, so it's difficult to balance everything on top. Also, shop-bought meringue can have a dustiness to it rather than the lovely chewiness of home-made. Give me home-made every time.

1 pink Florida grapefruit
150ml/5fl oz/⅔ cup double/heavy cream
1 tbsp icing/confectioners' sugar
1 tsp pink peppercorns, plus extra to serve
a few raspberries

For the meringue nests:
3 large egg whites, at room temperature
200g/7oz/scant 1 cup caster/superfine sugar
½ tsp cornflour/cornstarch
pink food colouring paste (optional)

For the sweet rocket drizzle:
30g/1oz rocket/arugula,
    plus a few extra leaves to serve
1½ tbsp icing/ confectioners' sugar

RECIPE CONTINUES OVERLEAF

First, make the meringue nests – you can skip this step if using shop-bought. Preheat the oven to 160°C/140°C fan/300°F/Gas 2 and line a large baking sheet with baking parchment. Draw four 12cm/5in circles on the parchment with a pencil.

Put the egg whites in the clean, grease-free bowl of a stand mixer fitted with a balloon whisk (or into a large bowl if you are using an electric hand whisk) and start whisking. Once the eggs are foamy, start adding the caster sugar, a spoonful at a time, making sure each spoonful is incorporated before adding the next. Once all the sugar is added, add the cornflour and keep whisking for a good 5 minutes until the meringue is firm and glossy – when you rub a little of the meringue between your thumb and forefinger, it shouldn't feel grainy at all.

Add a couple of drops of food colour paste (if using) and very roughly stir in with a spatula – you want swirls in the mixture. Divide the meringue evenly among the circles drawn on your baking sheet. Once you have an evenly sized pile in the middle of each circle, use a dessertspoon to spread the meringue out to the sides, creating nests with a dip in the middle.

Put the meringues in the oven and immediately turn the temperature down to 140°C/120°C fan/275°F/Gas 1. Cook for 1 hour, then turn the heat off and leave them to cool down in the oven (don't open the door).

To assemble the pavlovas, cut the top and bottom off the grapefruit, place on a board and slice the skin away by running your knife down the side from top to bottom. Curve your cut with the shape of the fruit so you don't lose any flesh. Cutting down each side of a membrane, slice the segments out of the fruit, leaving any tough membrane behind. Squeeze the remaining grapefruit membrane over a bowl to extract any juice left behind.

To make the drizzle, pop the rocket leaves, sugar and 1 tablespoon of the reserved grapefruit juice into a mini chopper or small bowl of a food processor and blitz to a smooth paste. You may need to stop and clean the sides of the chopper with a spatula to get it all to blend. Add the extra grapefruit juice or a little water if you need to, to get a smooth, loose paste. Leave it in the mini chopper while you assemble the rest.

Put the cream and icing sugar in a bowl and whisk until it is starting to thicken. Add the pink peppercorns, squashing them between your fingers as you go to break them up a little, and continue whipping the cream to soft peaks. Cream keeps thickening even after you stop whipping, so make sure you stop as soon as the cream is holding a peak or it will go too far and look grainy.

To assemble the pavlovas, place a meringue nest on each dessert plate. Divide the cream between the nests and top with the grapefruit slices and a few raspberries. Drizzle a little of the rocket drizzle over each one and finish with a sprinkling of pink peppercorns and a few dainty leaves of rocket.

WHITE FOREST PRETZEL CHEESECAKE

I've added salty pretzels and white chocolate to the biscuit base of this centrepiece dessert and a touch of juniper to the berry fruit swirl that punctuates the creamy white cheesecake layer to bring in another Eastern European flavouring. You encounter enlivening pops of berry gin cocktail flavour as you discover each pocket of berry coulis – delightful.

For the base:

100g/3½oz plain salted pretzels

100g/3½oz digestive biscuits

100g/3½oz unsalted butter

80g/3oz white chocolate, broken into pieces

For the topping:

1 tbsp dried juniper berries

5 sheets leaf gelatine

350g/12oz black forest frozen berry mix, defrosted, plus extra frozen berries for the top

100g/3½oz/generous ¾ cup icing/confectioners' sugar

250g/9oz mascarpone cheese

400g/14oz cream cheese

1½ tsp vanilla extract

To decorate:

30g/1oz white chocolate, broken into pieces

50g/2oz white chocolate fudge-covered pretzels

RECIPE CONTINUES OVERLEAF

Grease and line a 20cm/8in springform cake tin.

For the base, put the pretzels and digestives into a strong freezer bag and bash them to crumbs with a rolling pin – or blitz them in a food processor. Tip them into a mixing bowl. Melt the butter and white chocolate together – either in a bain marie or in the microwave – then stir it into the crumbs until evenly incorporated. Tip the mixture into the prepared tin and spread evenly, then press it down firmly (a potato masher is useful for this). Chill in the refrigerator until set.

To make the filling, put the juniper berries in a pestle and mortar and grind them coarsely. Put the gelatine sheets in a shallow bowl of cold water and leave them to soak for 5 minutes.

Meanwhile, put the defrosted berries into a bowl and use a stick blender to roughly blitz the berries to break them down a little – you still want plenty of texture in there. Place a fine-meshed sieve/strainer over a small saucepan and tip the berries into it. Once most of the liquid has drained away, tip the berries back into the bowl and stir in 30g/1oz/¼ cup of the icing sugar and the crushed juniper berries.

Heat the berry liquid in the pan gently. Once it is warm, squeeze out the gelatine sheets and add them to the pan. Stir over a very low heat until the gelatine has all dissolved, then turn the heat off and leave the mixture to cool a little.

Put the mascarpone, cream cheese, vanilla and the remaining icing sugar in the bowl of a stand mixer fitted with a balloon whisk (or use a mixing bowl and an electric hand whisk) and beat until smooth. Once it's no longer hot, pour in the berry gelatine mixture and mix again until smooth.

Remove the base from the refrigerator and layer up the berry and creamy mixtures on top, adding a blob of each and lightly mixing them together as you go, but making sure they are still distinct and swirled together in a pretty way. Smooth the top level and return the cheesecake to the refrigerator for a few hours, or preferably overnight, to set.

To decorate, melt the white chocolate gently in the microwave and use a spoon to drizzle it over the top of the cheesecake. Add the white pretzels around the outer rim of the cheesecake and finish with a final few frozen berries just before serving.

SMOKY BLACKSTRAP PUDDING

Liquid smoke extract intensifies the smoky treacle flavour of these sticky toffee puds. And I love the drama of serving a monochrome, almost black and white, pudding to my guests.

For a truly dramatic contrast, you could add a little black food colouring to the toffee sauce, as the vivid black sauce would look very striking against the white of the cream, but that's up to you. I think they look just gorgeous as they are.

150g/5oz pitted Medjool dates, roughly chopped
120ml/4fl oz/½ cup boiling water
75g/2½ oz unsalted butter, plus extra for greasing
60g/2¼oz/⅓ cup molasses sugar or
   dark muscovado/brown sugar
3 tbsp black treacle or blackstrap molasses
1 large egg
1 tsp vanilla extract
½ tsp liquid smoke extract
125g/4oz/1 cup self-raising flour
½ tsp bicarbonate of soda/baking soda
3 tbsp whole milk

For the sauce:
80g/3oz/scant ½ cup molasses sugar or
   dark muscovado/brown sugar
80g/3oz unsalted butter
200ml/7fl oz/scant 1 cup double/heavy cream,
   plus extra to serve
2 tbsp black treacle or blackstrap molasses
1 tsp liquid smoke extract, or to taste (this will depend
   on how concentrated your smoke extract is)
black food colouring (optional)

Put the dates in a bowl and add the boiling water. Cover and leave to soak for about 30 minutes.

Meanwhile, preheat the oven to 200°C/180°C fan/400°F/Gas 6 and generously grease four (180ml/6fl oz/¾ cup volume) ramekins or dariole moulds.

In a stand mixer fitted with a paddle attachment, beat together the butter and sugar for several minutes until light and fluffy, then mix in the treacle.

Beat the egg in a jug with the vanilla and smoke extract. Sift the flour and bicarbonate of soda onto a plate. Add half of the egg to the butter and sugar mixture and beat in followed by half the flour and beat again. Repeat to add the remaining egg and flour, then beat in the milk.

Use a fork to mash the soaked dates to a chunky purée, then fold them into the batter. Divide the batter among the four greased moulds and place them on a baking sheet. Transfer to the oven and bake for about 25 minutes until risen.

To make the toffee sauce, put the all the ingredients into a saucepan set over a low heat and stir until everything has dissolved. Increase the heat and bring to the boil for a minute or so until the mixture has thickened to a thick sauce. (If you would like to bump up the black smoky look, add a little black food colouring at this point.)

Place each pudding in a serving bowl and pour the sauce over. Finish with a drizzle of double cream.

EARL GREY POSSETS
WITH LEMON AND CORIANDER SHORTBREAD

An elegant little dessert, these creamy tea-flavoured possets are so easy to make. They are perfectly complemented by the delicate lemon and coriander-seed shortbreads, which are also a doddle to prepare. The shortbread quantity could easily be doubled – if you're going to the trouble of hand-making, you may as well make more and keep in a tin to nibble when the mood takes you.

For the possets:
600ml/20fl oz/2½ cups double/heavy cream
4 good-quality Earl Grey tea bags
200g/7oz/scant 1 cup caster/superfine sugar

For the shortbread:
2 tsp coriander seeds
50g/2oz unsalted butter, softened
30g/1oz/2 tbsp caster/superfine sugar,
   plus extra for the tops
finely grated zest of 1 lemon
85g/3oz/¾ cup plain/all-purpose flour,
   plus extra for dusting

Put the cream and tea bags in a saucepan and warm gently over a low heat. Remove from the heat and leave to cool and infuse for about 20 minutes.

Leave the tea bags in the cream and add the sugar to the pan. Place over a low heat again and stir until the sugar dissolves. Increase the heat and bring the cream to the boil, then boil for 3 minutes before removing from the heat. Remove the tea bags and leave to cool down a little before pouring into four pretty tea cups. Chill for at least 5 hours, or ideally overnight, until set.

While the possets are chilling, make the shortbread. Preheat the oven to 200°C/180°C fan/400°F/Gas 6 and line a baking sheet with baking parchment.

Put the coriander seeds on a separate lipped baking sheet and toast lightly in the oven for 5 minutes or so as the oven heats up, then coarsely grind the seeds in a pestle and mortar to release the flavour, but don't grind too finely.

Cream the butter and sugar together until light and fluffy. Add the coriander seeds and lemon zest and beat again to fully incorporate the aromatics. Sift the flour into the bowl and mix to a firm dough.

Roll out the dough on a lightly floured surface until it is about 5mm/¼in thick. Using a cookie cutter, stamp out biscuits from the dough and place them on the prepared baking sheet. Prick them lightly with a fork, then bake for 15–20 minutes until light golden.

Sprinkle a little extra sugar on a plate, then once the biscuits have cooled for a minute or so to set, turn them upside down onto the sugar to cover the tops. Leave them to cool on a wire/cooling rack.

Once the possets have chilled and the biscuits have cooled, serve them together.

ALMOND ANGOSTURA GRANITA

Angostura bitters, in its iconic bottle with over-sized label, is an aromatic classic of the cocktail cabinet. With a gentle herbal flavour based on gentian and numerous herbs and spices, it is one of Trinidad and Tobago's most recognisable exports. I've used the bitters here to flavour a light, creamy, dairy-free granita. An icy treat to end a long hot summer's day, it is a lovely dish for entertaining.

600ml/20fl oz/2½ cups unsweetened almond milk drink
80g/3oz/⅓ cup soft light brown sugar
1 tbsp Angostura bitters
2 tsp finely grated orange zest, plus extra to serve

Put the almond milk in a wide, shallow, freezer-proof container with a lid (an old ice cream tub is good) and stir in the sugar, bitters and orange zest. Pop the lid on and place the container in the freezer for 2 hours.

Remove the container from the freezer and use a fork to break up the ice that will have begun forming around the edges of the tub. Return the tub to the freezer.

After another hour, remove the tub and, again, use a fork to break up the ice crystals. Repeat this process two or three times more, stirring with a fork each hour, until the whole mixture is frozen into small loose crystals.

To serve, spoon the granita into four glass serving bowls, dividing it evenly among them. Sprinkle with the curls of pared orange zest, and serve immediately.

RAINFOREST
REFRESHER

I'm taking you to India by way of Mexico here with a tropical street salad with a twist. This unusual salad makes a perfect dessert for those who don't like things that are too sugary (like me). After a meal, serving a simple plate of fresh fruit is not uncommon in India, and in Northern India it will often be sprinkled with a more unusual ingredient – black salt, or *kala namak*. Something of an acquired taste, it is a pungent kiln-fired rock salt with a fermented flavour. You can leave it out if it's not to your taste.

Sweet ripe papaya is here complemented by creamy avocado, and the hit of red chilli pepper makes things really interesting. Chilli in dessert is alone a bold move; adding black salt is for the intrepid who want to take the boldness up a notch.

juice of 2 limes
1 tbsp honey
1 small papaya
2 avocados
½ red chilli, sliced into rings
a few small fresh mint leaves
black salt, to sprinkle (optional)

Combine the lime juice and honey in a small bowl, mixing until the honey has dissolved, and set aside.

Peel the papaya, then halve it and scrape out the seeds. Slice it into slim wedges and arrange them on a serving platter. Halve the avocados, remove the pits and peel, and slice those into slim wedges too. Add to the serving platter with the papaya.

Drizzle the honey and lime dressing all over the fruit, then scatter with the red chilli and mint leaves. If you are feeling very brave, add a few pinches of the black salt and serve immediately.

SESAME SPICED FLAPJACKS

These yummy, moreish snack bars take the humble flapjack to a more savoury dimension, a sort-of cross between an oaty flapjack and the snappy sesame bars so popular around the Mediterranean and Middle East. Aromatic Chinese five-spice and the toasty notes of sesame oil make these an altogether more grown-up treat that are a little less sweet and a lot more interesting for your elevenses or mid-afternoon snack attack. You can cut these into whatever size suits you and they store well in an airtight tin.

180g/6½oz salted butter, plus extra for greasing
50g/2oz/⅓ cup sesame seeds (feel free to use
   a mixture of 50/50 white and black)
1 tbsp golden syrup
2 tbsp sesame oil
160g/5½oz/¾ cup light soft brown sugar
1 tbsp Chinese 5-spice powder
425g/15oz/3⅓ cups porridge/rolled oats
a pinch of salt

Preheat the oven to 200°C/180°C fan/400°F/Gas 6. Grease a 20 x 30cm/8 x 12in brownie tin with a little butter and line with baking parchment.

Tip the sesame seeds onto a baking sheet and toast them in the oven for about 5 minutes, or until they are golden and smelling toasty. Keep an eye on them as they can burn easily and remove them from the hot baking sheet as soon as they come out the oven or they will keep cooking.

Meanwhile, put the butter in a saucepan and set over a low–medium heat to melt. Once melted, stir in the golden syrup and toasted sesame oil, then add the sugar and 5-spice powder. Add the oats, toasted sesame seeds and a good pinch of salt to the saucepan and stir until everything is really well mixed. Tip the mixture into the prepared baking tin and spread level, then press the mixture down firmly – a potato masher is useful for this.

Cook the flapjacks for about 25 minutes, or until golden on top. Leave them to cool and set in the tin, then tip them out onto a board and slice into squares or bars to serve. They will keep for up to a week in an airtight container.

HALVA AND
ROSE COOKIES

Elevate this easy-but-basic cookie recipe with a delicious Middle-Eastern-inspired blend of rose with delicately flavoured sesame halva. You could really use any flavour of halva you like (and replace the rose flavour with another), but I find honey-flavoured halva works beautifully. An elegant accompaniment to a strong coffee or perhaps a mint tea, these pretty little biscuits can be served either slightly warm or cold.

120g/4oz unsalted butter
160g/5½oz/¾ cup golden caster/superfine sugar
½ tsp rose water (or more depending on the strength of your brand)
1 tsp vanilla extract
1 small egg
200g/7oz/1⅔ cups self-raising flour
2 tbsp edible dried rose petals (optional – try the tea section in health food stores)
90g/3¼oz honey-flavoured (or vanilla-flavoured) halva, chopped into 12 equal-sized squares

Put the butter and sugar in a large bowl, or in the bowl of a stand mixer fitted with a paddle, and beat together until light and fluffy. Add the rose water and vanilla extract, and beat in, then beat in the egg.

Sift the flour into the bowl and fold in with a spatula until the mixture starts to come together into a dough. Add the dried rose petals now, if using, and continue to bring it into a ball with your hands. Divide the dough into 12 equal portions and roll into balls.

Line two baking sheets with baking parchment and place six balls on each sheet, spacing them well apart as the cookies will spread. Press them down a little to make patties, then press a square of halva into the centre of each one. Place in the refrigerator to chill for 30 minutes.

Meanwhile, preheat the oven to 200°C/180°C fan/ 400°F/Gas 6.

Once the cookies have chilled, bake the sheets, one at a time, for about 13 minutes, or until light golden brown. Leave the cookies to set on the baking sheets for a few minutes before serving warm, or move to a wire/cooling rack to cool completely.

DRINKS

MAYAN HOT CHOCOLATE

The ancient Mayans were the originators of what we know today as hot chocolate, believing it a gift from the gods (what changes?!). Their *xocolatl* was a bitter water-based drink made with crushed cocoa, cornmeal and chilli pepper. Try adding some authentic spices and chilli to your hot chocolate for a bold kick to this rich, silky treat. All of the spices I've used here would have been available to the Mayans. Morita chillies have an intense smoky flavour – you could use chilli powder at a push, but the flavour won't be as complex or delicious.

100g/3½oz dark/bittersweet chocolate (85% cocoa solids or higher), plus extra, grated, to decorate
600ml/20fl oz/2½ cups whole milk
finely grated zest of 1 large orange
1 tsp natural vanilla extract
½ tsp ground allspice
1 tbsp runny honey
1 dried chipotle morita chilli

Chop the chocolate into small pieces and place it in a saucepan. Add the milk, orange zest, vanilla, allspice and honey. Slice the chilli in half and add that too. Cook the hot chocolate over a low heat, stirring constantly, until the chocolate has melted and the mixture is homogeneous. Taste, and if you'd like it hotter, leave it over the heat for a little longer for the chilli to infuse more heat, but don't let it boil.

Pour the hot chocolate through a sieve/fine-mesh strainer into a jug, then divide it evenly among four small mugs. Sprinkle over a little more grated chocolate to decorate. Enjoy hot.

AVO, BASIL AND COCONUT LASSI

This unusual combination of flavours makes a refreshing lassi for hot weather. It particularly makes a great breakfast smoothie as it it is substantial enough to set you up for the day.

It's optional, but you could top with a little desiccated/dried shredded coconut too, for an attractive effect if serving to guests. It's very rich, so serve in small glasses.

½ large avocado, peeled and pitted
150ml/5fl oz/⅔ cup whole milk
100g/3½oz/generous ⅓ cup coconut yogurt
2 tbsp lime juice
2 tsp honey
a small handful of fresh basil

Put the avocado, milk, yogurt, lime juice and honey into a blender and blitz until smooth. Add a splash of cold water to loosen if it is too thick.

Set aside a couple of the small basil sprigs for garnish and add the rest of the basil to the blender. Blitz into the lassi, leaving a few flecks unblended for a bit of visual interest, if you like.

Pour the mixture evenly between two glasses, top each with a basil sprig and serve.

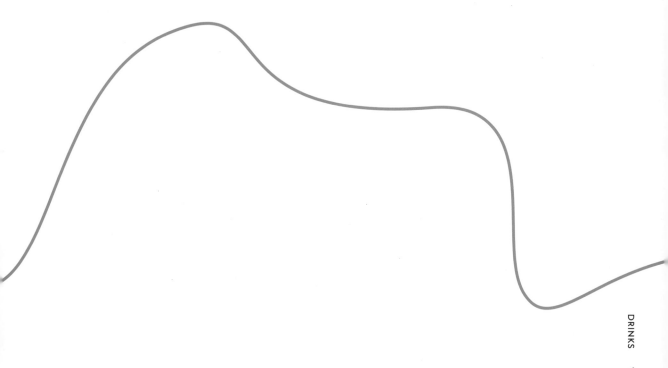

ROASTED CORN AND ELDERFLOWER ICED TEA

You can get Korean roasted corn tea from Asian supermarkets or online – it tastes a little like drinking popcorn. It combines perfectly with the flavours of elderflower and mint for a beautifully aromatic cool drink. If you want to serve it as a cocktail to evening guests, you can switch the elderflower cordial for St Germain liqueur.

2 Korean roasted corn tea bags
120ml/4fl oz/½ cup elderflower cordial
ice cubes and sprigs of fresh mint, to serve

Put the tea bags in a jug and top up with 1 litre/35fl oz/4¼ cups cold water. Place in the refrigerator for several hours to chill – the longer you leave it, the stronger the corn flavour will get.

Once the tea has chilled (and infused the water in the process), add the elderflower cordial.

To serve, fill four highball glasses with ice cubes and pour in the tea, then garnish with the mint sprigs.

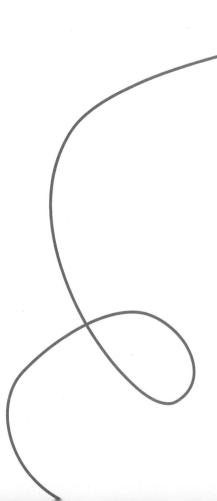

LIME AND
THYME FIZZ

A twist on the classic Gin Fizz cocktail, this elegant tipple uses fresh thyme for a gorgeously summery, herbal flavour.

A little tip for measuring egg whites (particularly if they are very fresh): once you have separated your egg, whisking the egg white with a fork will break it up and make it much easier to measure out.

1 lime
50ml/1¾fl oz/3 tbsp plus 1 tsp gin
15ml/½fl oz/1 tbsp simple sugar syrup (store-bought)
2 large sprigs of fresh thyme, plus a dainty
   sprig to serve
25ml/¾fl oz/1 tbsp plus 2 tsp egg white
   (see tip above for measuring)
2 large ice cubes
25ml/¾fl oz/1 tbsp plus 2 tsp soda water

Pare the peel off half of the lime and pop it in a cocktail shaker. Using a microplane or other fine grater, zest the other half of the lime and set the grated zest aside. Slice the lime in half and squeeze the juice from it.

To the shaker with the lime peel, add 25ml/¾fl oz/ 1 tablespoon plus 2 teaspoons of the squeezed lime juice along with the gin, sugar syrup, thyme and egg white. Dry shake (without ice) for 20 seconds to whip up a good froth. Add the ice to the shaker and shake for about 10 seconds, or until there's a frost on the shaker.

Strain the cocktail into a glass and top up with the soda water. Garnish with a line of finely grated lime zest and a dainty sprig of thyme. Allow the drink to sit for a few seconds until the foam separates and rises to the top for that classic layered look of a good Gin Fizz.

ZINGY GINGER AND TAMARIND MARGARITA

The tamarind and ginger here give the classic Margarita some spicy, tangy background notes. Sadly, both ginger and tamarind don't have the most attractive colour in the world, but what they lack in looks, they make up for in zing. An audacious drink for the bold of heart.

Tip: For a more clarified look to your cocktail, try putting it through a paper coffee filter after the first (dry) shake to remove any very fine sediment from the tamarind paste, before adding it back to the shaker with the ice.

25ml/¾fl oz/1 tbsp plus 2 tsp fresh lime juice
50ml/1¾fl oz/3 tbsp plus 1 tsp tequila
25ml/¾fl oz/1 tbsp plus 2 tsp triple sec
½ tsp smooth tamarind paste
a chunk of fresh root ginger, chopped and bashed
2 large ice cubes

For the glass garnish:
flaky sea salt
a slice each of lime and ginger

Start by garnishing your glass. Tip a little salt onto a small plate. Run the lime slice around the rim of a coupe glass to dampen it, then invert the glass onto the salt. Once the rim is covered, leave it to dry while you make the cocktail.

Put the lime juice, tequila, triple sec, tamarind paste and bashed ginger pieces into a cocktail shaker and dry shake (without ice) for 20 seconds to extract flavour from the ginger (you have the option to strain the liquid through a paper coffee filter here, if wished – see tip, left – then return the cocktail to the shaker). Add the ice to the shaker and shake for about 10 seconds, or until there's a frost on the shaker.

Strain the cocktail into your prepared glass and garnish the rim further with a slice of ginger and lime.

INDEX

THANK
YOU

So many thanks to everyone who was involved in the making of this book.

I am forever indebted to the amazing team at Watkins, particularly Fiona Robertson, my publisher, who planted the seed of this idea and helped it grow.

Such a big thank you to my editor Emily Preece-Morrison, without whom I could not put pen to paper – you are very much the motivator and fire in my writing belly.

Thank you to the wonderful Becci Woods, who is my sister of flavour, my twin soul when it comes to what makes the world taste delicious. Thanks also to Tamara Vos for tasting and testing and tasting again.

And a huge thank you to the army who worked behind the scenes to bring this beautiful book into the world. To Georgie Hewitt, designer extraordinaire, who brought both style to the pages and organised and art directed the photoshoot to perfection; to Martin Poole, photographic maestro and chief sticky-toffee-pudding eater (and for putting up with whippets on set!); to Hannah Wilkinson for understanding exactly the look I wanted ('Liverpool chic' is now a thing!); to Kim Morphew for styling the food gorgeously (in a heatwave); to Kathy Steer for her meticulous checking; to Hilary Bird for indexing; to Karen Smith for in-house design support; to Uzma Taj for production; and finally to Andy Mountfield for yet more tasting and for kindly donating your family recipe.

Nisha Katona

BOLD
Nisha Katona

First published in the UK and USA in 2024 by
Nourish, an imprint of Watkins Media Limited
Unit 11, Shepperton House, 83–93 Shepperton Road
London N1 3DF

enquiries@nourishbooks.com

Publisher: Fiona Robertson
Project Editor: Emily Preece-Morrison
Head of Design: Karen Smith
Art Director & Lead Designer: Georgina Hewitt
Production: Uzma Taj
Commissioned Photography: Martin Poole
Recipe Development & Testing: Rebecca Woods
Additional Food Testing: Tamara Vos
Food Stylist: Kim Morphew
Prop Stylist: Hannah Wilkinson
Proofreader: Kathy Steer
Indexer: Hilary Bird

A CIP record for this book is available from the British Library

ISBN: 978-1-84899-423-2 (Hardback)
ISBN: 978-1-84899-426-3 (eBook)

10 9 8 7 6 5 4 3 2 1

Colour reproduction by Rival Colour
Printed in China

MIX
Paper from
responsible sources
FSC® C005748

Notes on the recipes
Unless otherwise stated:
Use medium fruit and vegetables
Use medium (US large) organic or free-range eggs
Use fresh herbs, spices and chillies
Use granulated sugar (Americans can use ordinary granulated
sugar when caster sugar is specified)
Do not mix metric, imperial and US cup measurements:
1 tsp = 5ml 1 tbsp = 15ml 1 cup = 240ml

nourishbooks.com